INDIAN-ISH

RECIPES AND ANTICS
FROM A MODERN
AMERICAN FAMILY

Priya Krishna

with Ritu Krishna

Photography by Mackenzie Kelley
Illustrations by Maria Qamar

Foreword by Padma Lakshmi

HOUGHTON MIFFLIN HARCOURT
BOSTON NEW YORK

hmhbooks.com

Library of Congress Cataloging-in-Publication Data
Names: Krishna, Priya, author. | Krishna, Ritu, author.
Title: Indian-ish : recipes and antics from a modern American family /
Priya Krishna with Ritu Krishna ; photography by Mackenzie Kelly ;
illustrations by Maria Qamar.
Description: Boston : Houghton Mifflin Harcourt, 2019. | Includes index. |
Identifiers: LCCN 2018043605 (print) | LCCN 2018044779 (ebook) | ISBN
9781328484321 (ebook) | ISBN 9781328482471 (paper over board)
Subjects: LCSH: Cooking, Indic. | Indian cooking. | Cooking—United States.
|LCGFT: Cookbooks.
Classification: LCC TX724.5.I4 (ebook) | LCC TX724.5.I4 K725 2019 (print) |
DDC 641.59/297—dc23
LC record available at https://lccn.loc.gov/2018043605

Book design by Kara Plikaitis
Food styling by Judy Kim

Printed in the United States of America

DOW 10 9 8 7 6 5 4
4500772513

To Mom and Dad

I must warn you. This is not a cookbook of traditional Indian food. It's not even a book about regional Indian specialties (if you're looking for that, please see *India* by Pushpesh Pant). India is a vast country, with many tribes, numerous languages (not just dialects), and various religions, modes of dress, customs, and ethnicities. People of Indian descent total over 1.2 billion across the globe, most of us running around contradicting one another. So there can never really be one definitive cookbook encompassing what all of us brown folk eat (again, except for Mr. Pant's). If you're looking for that, I'm sorry—you've bought the wrong book! But, the good news: You *have* bought a very interesting and delicious collection of extremely easy-to-make recipes from a mostly vegetarian Indian family in Dallas, Texas, that gives you a good idea of how many Indian immigrants in the United States eat today.

My family was like Priya's: Her mom, Ritu, working full time while also raising Priya and her sister reminds me of my own full-time working mom (except we didn't have Priya's dad to do the dishes!). These intrepid ladies moved to a new country, not really knowing what to expect, nor how they'd survive or even where to get curry leaves. They raised their kids with their heritage somewhat intact, acclimated in the way that most immigrants do, and made a fulfilling life for themselves. What has sprung forth from this wave of immigration from the Indian subcontinent during the 1970s to 1990s is a new cuisine that allows for wacky things like using olive oil (even though olives don't traditionally grow in India), making pizza with rotis, and baking eggless cakes to accommodate their Hindu vegetarianism. (Having said that, over seventy thousand olive trees have been transplanted from Israel to North India in the last ten years to help Rajasthani farmers, so maybe the Krishnas were just ahead of their time!) *Indian-ish* makes room for some very nontraditional ingredients because, at its heart, it still exemplifies the flavor principles of Indian food, making it accessible for today's American cook.

Foreword by Padma Lakshmi

So, while our grandmothers may have done it differently, to say that this cuisine is not authentic is missing the point. (I have a lot of trouble with the word "authentic," even if I do understand the way in which many people bandy it about.) This cuisine is indeed authentic, and while it may not be traditional Indian food or what we think of as American food, most of the over two million Indian-Americans in the United States would argue that it's actually both. What's more important, dear reader, is that it is a great starter book for anyone who has ever wondered how to make basic Indian food in an American kitchen. Priya and Ritu's methods are approachable, easy to execute, and employ everything from microwaves to Instant Pots, because that is the way most Americans do things now.

This cookbook is really a love letter from Priya to her mother, and when you peruse the pages, you will see why. But it is also so much more. It demystifies a very sophisticated and layered cuisine into something that's very doable—not only for a dinner party but also for a quick, yummy weeknight meal. You can pretty much get all the spices and odd Indian ingredients you need with one visit or online order to an Indian grocer (like Patel Brothers), so there's no longer any excuse to be intimidated. It turns out that all the hacks a busy suburban working mom of North Indian descent uses in her own kitchen in Dallas just happen to distill Indian home cooking to its essence, all while tying it to its new American roots. Master the simple recipes in this book (and they are very easy to master), and you'll know enough to understand the flavors that are common to most Indian food. Priya's easy directions walk you through every step, her humor will encourage you, and her suggestions will come in handy for other totally unrelated recipes you may encounter in your life.

I've known Priya for several years—I've watched her quit her job, become a real full-time writer, and blossom in all sorts of ways. She has inherited her mother's ambition and is every bit as intrepid, accomplishing whatever she sets her mind to do. So I am sure this cookbook will be a valuable addition to your kitchen, and your cooking repertoire will be the better for it. It will allow you to say you now know how to cook Indian food, even if you have to add the "-ish" when you serve her mother's olive tapenade next to the saag paneer made with feta. Happy cooking!

Contents

A lot of people say their moms are the best. But my mom, Ritu Krishna, is actually the best.

Introduction

Being a food writer is a Very. Cool. Job. I'm not going to be all coy and tell you otherwise! It's awesome! I've been fortunate to clock in a lot of hours of very delicious eating and drinking—in New York, where I spend most of my time, and elsewhere. Yes, my acid reflux is constantly acting up, and unpredictable digestive problems are just a state of mind. But aside from being CEO of the YKK zipper company (look at all the zippers on your pants—this brand has a monopoly on the fastening business!!!), there's no job I'd rather be doing than the one I am.

That said, the best part of my trajectory as a food writer hasn't necessarily been the meals (though, can I brag for a moment and say that I have taken shots with Bill Murray, and had chai with Madhur Jaffrey, for journalism??)—but rather how, in the process, I have finally been able to come to terms with my roots. Specifically, I have realized that my mom is simply the coolest.

You see, a lot of people say their moms are the best. But my mom, Ritu Krishna, is actually the best. Remember when Sheryl Sandberg first started urging people to lean in, and people treated this like a brand-new idea? Far before that was happening, my mom was blazing the trail in our family for how to be a successful mom and working woman, all while pursuing many side hustles and being an awesome, creative force in the kitchen.

Whenever I eat at any restaurant, whether it is a highly-sought-after taco stand or some heavily awarded sushi restaurant, I find myself constantly craving my mom's food. I leave incredible meals hankering for my mom's roti pizza, served in a plate she bought from a street vendor in Lima, alongside a glass of wine she has especially chosen for the occasion.

Let me back up to my childhood. As a kid in Dallas, I was lucky enough to be surrounded by an enormous Indian family—my dad, my sister, my mom, her brothers, their spouses, and their kids, all of whom lived no more than a twenty-minute car ride away. But outside the comfortable cocoon of our family and close friends, I felt more defined by what I *wasn't* than what I was.

At the very liberal (and mostly Jewish) school I attended, I ended up hanging out with 99 percent white people—ironically, one of the only other Indian girls in my class bullied me. Most of my friends had straightened brown hair (mine was black and frizzy); ate turkey-and-mustard sandwiches for lunch (Mom packed me dal until I begged her to switch to PB&Js); wore crystal-studded 7 for All Mankind A-pocket jeans (my parents refused to spend $200 on a pair of jeans that poked you when you sat down); vacationed at Atlantis, the Bahamas beach resort made famous by the Olsen twins (aside from watching *Holiday in the Sun* a hundred times, I did no such thing); and held their bat mitzvahs at the Columbian Country Club in Carrollton (obviously this was not possible for me).

After college, I worked for a phenomenal but now defunct food magazine called *Lucky Peach*, where I went from being the customer service person who picked up the phone when you need to change your subscriber address (an excellent way to learn people skills, *fast*) to overseeing all marketing and events.

I eventually left to pursue my interest in reporting, and I've since gotten to write for outlets that previously felt far outside the realm of possibility for me: the *New York Times*, *Bon Appétit*, the *New Yorker*, and the like. And after years of rejecting the food and culture of my people, the place I've found myself turning to for inspiration is my mom: how she came up with a foolproof formula for making dal; the many ways she makes chai; why the Indian grocery store she and my dad frequent is really worth the drive.

About half the stories I write either center on my family, or are the product of ideas given to me by my family. All the things that made me the awkward kid in school who didn't eat and dress like everyone else—*those* have become my strengths as a writer. At some point, that deep shame and desire to hide who I was morphed into something resembling confidence.

My mom grew up in India at a time when women weren't expected to pursue a career other than being a mother. Instead, she moved to America, married my dad (more on him soon), put herself through college by folding clothes at Sears, and became a software programmer and eventually the manager for an airline software company—a job that allowed her to pursue her dream of traveling the world. She never learned to cook growing up, but she did spend a lot of time watching her grandmother make dinner. So when she immigrated to the United States, she watched tons of PBS cooking shows, and melded those techniques with her memories of her grandmother's food, the best dishes she had eaten while traveling, and, of course, the requests of her two needy daughters who were very much products of American culture and demanded spaghetti and pizza every night.

For as long as I can remember, my mom has felt wise beyond any age. She has taught me about the importance of statement jewelry, why *Shall We Dance?* (the Richard Gere version) is one of the most significant movies of our time, the right way to ask for a raise at work, and the proper method for folding a pair of pants (one day, my mom made my sister and I fold one hundred consecutive pairs of pants so we'd never forget).

And while I was busy being an angsty teen, my mom was performing culinary wizardry in our kitchen every night. She was making pizzas out of roti (an ingenious trick for a crispy crust every time), cooking saag paneer with feta cubes instead of paneer, and turning leftover sabzi into portable, travel-size Indian taquitos. My mom studied software engineering because that was the known entity to her at the time. But had she grown up in a different culture, I bet she would have worked in food.

And if that wasn't enough, my mother also (putting this in bullets for ~dramatic effect~):

- Managed the team that wrote the software for the first self-service check-in machines at airports

- Help launched a film festival dedicated to works by South Asians

- Started her own movie review hashtag on Twitter (#RitusReviews)

- Became a style icon (seriously, she is complimented on her outfit no fewer than ten times a day)

- Hiked the gosh darn Inca Trail with no previous hiking experience

- Taught herself a sommelier-level understanding of wine

- INSPIRED HER YOUNGEST DAUGHTER (ME) TO WRITE A BOOK

Which brings me to where we are now. Hello! Welcome to *Indian-ish*. This is a book about me, and about my mom, told through her one-of-a-kind recipes. It's the best of both of us: my outlandish tales and lack of shame, plus her food.

Indian-ish was never supposed to be the title of this book. It was actually the placeholder title I put on the book proposal until I could think of something better. But I slowly started realizing that the word is actually the perfect encapsulation of my life and my relationship to my family.

First and foremost, Indian-ish describes my mom's cooking— 60 percent traditional Indian, 40 percent Indian-plus-something else, mostly vegetarian—like a South Indian–meets–Spanish tomato rice topped with broiled cheddar cheese, sandwiches crusted with pan-fried curry leaves, and the like. There are even a few recipes that will straight-up not feel Indian at all—like Anvita's Dump Cake (page 207), or Lima Bean and Basil Dip (page 52). But they all equally comprise our family's unique culinary canon.

But *Indian-ish* is also about identity—that feeling of talking and thinking and acting like an American, but looking like an Indian. Part of two worlds, but never *fully* part of one. *Indian-ish* is the Hindi-English hybrid language my family speaks at home; my mom pairing her kurtas from New Delhi with gold pants from Zara; our family toting sabzi taquitos onto planes because we don't want to subject ourselves to the in-flight food; my dad blasting the *Kabhi Khushi Kabhie Gham*

soundtrack in the car instead of Top 40 hits. *Indian-ish* is my parents coming to America in 1980 with very little, and finding a way to thrive through their tenacity and work ethic without losing sight of where they came from. This is who we are—and you know what? I'm so proud of who I am.

This book is a family project as much as it is my project. It's the result of my mom writing one hundred (!!!!) recipes after stressful workdays; my dad doing hundreds of dishes wearing nothing but a *lungi* (Google it); my uncles and aunts rearranging their work schedules so they could help me write down *their* recipes; my sister, Meera, and brother-in-law, David (and 100+ others!) testing endless recipes; and my parents opening their house and their belongings so we could photograph this cookbook and make a huge mess of their kitchen every single day for two weeks.

Most important, though, the recipes in here are really, really good. Each and every one of these dishes was tested by my mom, me, and three friends with varying degrees of cooking abilities. I cut the ones that got mixed reviews (the recipes, not the friends), and only kept in the greatest hits. You're getting the cream of the crop of my mom's culinary treasury. Which is fantastic, because my mom is a genius.

Now, repeat after me: INDIAN FOOD IS EVERYDAY FOOD. Instead of a meat and two sides, I grew up on dal, rice (or roti), sabzi (sautéed vegetables), and salad—dishes that come together quickly (Can you chop vegetables? You can make Indian food!), fill you up (protein, baby!), taste decidedly complex, and (with the exception of salad) keep really well as leftovers.

If Indian food were actually hard to make, would billions of working Indian parents be whipping it up on the regular for their weeknight dinners? No. Indian food is honestly really straightforward. I could probably boil it down to "Heat oil in a pan, throw in spices, probably onions, too, add vegetables or rice or lentils, and you're done!" YES, okay, that is a gross generalization of a cuisine that is breathtaking in its diversity, but you get the idea. (That said, check out the flowchart on page 37 for my vastly oversimplified visual guide to making Indian food.)

Also, the dishes in this book are specifically built to be an *accessible* entry point into Indian cuisine—mainly because my mom is busy, and she does not have the time to slave away at the stove all day. You'll never see a recipe that calls for dozens of different spices, asks you to spend the entire day standing over a pot, or uses highly technical cooking terminology—mainly because that's not how my mom cooks, and that's not how I cook. If my very lazy self can make all this stuff, so can you! Soon you'll be churning out a casual Red Pepper, Potato, and

Peanut Sabzi (page 93) after a long day of work and being all, "Oh, what, this? Just something I whipped up!" These recipes will become as intuitive for you to cook on a weeknight as they are for my mom . . . or, at the very least, as they are for me. (We can't all be as fabulous as my mom.)

I hope this book does well, largely so that publishers and consumers will take more chances on stories like this one, which don't fit the mold of what has dominated the cookbook genre for so long—a mostly whitewashed interpretation of America and its food. I wish for a day when dal chawal is as normalized a Monday night meal as spaghetti or grilled chicken.

So—here's to being the awkward Indian kid with overplucked eyebrows and crippling insecurities. I'll take comfort in the fact that being told my lunchbox smelled like "rotten curry" served the larger purpose of getting me a book deal. This one's for you, Ma.

***Almost all the dishware featured in this book is from my mom's personal collection, the result of many years of international travel.

FAQs

Why should I make Indian food at home? I am still very skeptical. The Mumbai Curry Xpress down the street from my house serves amazing chicken tikka masala! You should really try it!

I have a lot of thoughts, but my main one is this: The vast majority of menus served at Indian restaurants like your "Mumbai Curry Xpress" are dominated by a category of Indian food, born during the Mughal Empire, that's laden with rich, gravy-based meat and vegetable stews. Because these restaurants serve more or less the same menu, the general perception is that Indian food is "heavy" or "too complicated" or "too rich" or "makes me poop like crazy" (though the last one is not entirely incorrect, since lentils are very high in fiber). The Indian food you'll find cooked in people's homes is nothing like that—it's heavily regional, each dish's spice composition is unique, and, like in every cuisine, there is a mixture of light, everyday foods and richer indulgences. Make Indian food at home, using fresh, *whole* spices, and you'll realize that Indian cooking is (1) not that time-consuming; (2) great for affordable everyday meals; and (3) generally pretty healthy.

Why are there no curries in this book?

Let me get another big misconception out of the way. THERE IS NO SUCH THING AS CURRY—at least not the way you might know it. Yes, there are curry leaves, which are great, and stews called *kadhi* (page 157), which kind of sounds like "curry." But the term was largely popularized by Europeans during their colonization of India as a homogeneous catchall for the various stews they encountered in Indian cuisine. If you don't want to sound like a tone-deaf person when talking about Indian food, just refer to the dishes by their actual names.

What do you mean by "small," "medium," and "large" onions/tomatoes/potatoes in your recipes? What if I don't know what that means and get the wrong size?

Think of a small onion/tomato/potato as being about the size of your fist; medium the size of a tennis ball; and large the size of a softball. All that said, the beauty of the recipes in this book (and of most Indian food, in general) is that they are extremely forgiving. Use your best judgment on size, but if your potatoes are slightly larger or your tomatoes slightly smaller, it is *okay*. The recipe will still turn out just fine.

What if I burn my cumin, or any spices for that matter?

Dump it out, rinse the pan, and try again. Burning spices is practically a rite of passage when making Indian food (just ask my dad, who had to scrub our pots with steel wool at least a dozen times during my recipe-testing process at home). You'll probably do it once or twice, but then you'll never do it again! The most foolproof way to prevent burnt spices? Keep the heat low, and immediately take the pan off the heat if you catch even a slight whiff of burning.

Can I use canned tomatoes instead of fresh ones?

Only if you have to. I had a lot of recipe testers tell me they used canned tomatoes because they couldn't find good tomatoes in the dead of winter. I like a good canned tomato as much as the next person, but I have found that even those sad fresh winter tomatoes seem to work better in bringing that necessary brightness to Indian dishes than canned ones. And I don't love the metallic taste that cans add to tomatoes. I am of course in full support of buying local and in season whenever you can, but . . . if you can stomach buying a couple of fresh tomatoes when you're cooking these recipes in the winter, your dish will probably be better off.

Why do all the instructions call for Roma tomatoes? Why that variety? And aren't they the same thing as plum tomatoes?

Yes, Roma tomatoes and plum tomatoes are the same thing. My family and I are just used to seeing them labeled as Roma tomatoes at our grocery stores. We love Roma tomatoes for their very distinct flavor—they've got a little more tang and tartness than non-Roma varietals, which adds that fresh, enlivening component to Indian food. If you're in love with another variety, feel free to use it, but know that these recipes were made with Romas in mind!

When I'm using cilantro, should I discard the stems?

Most of the time, we use both the stems and the leaves—the stems have just as much flavor, and because of their water content, they add an extra shot of that cilantro-y brightness. There are a few recipes, though, where only the leaves are used (often for aesthetic reasons), and I've specified as such.

What are your thoughts on peeling things?

In general, I'm a lazy cook. I don't peel things unless I absolutely have to. Also, I genuinely like unpeeled vegetables—the skin has fiber, and it usually lends a nice, crisp texture to whatever you're cooking. Using the skin cuts down on food waste, too. In this book, I have specified if a vegetable needs to be peeled, but in general, don't feel the need to be obsessively peeling every piece of ginger or stick of carrot.

If a recipe calls for "ghee or olive oil," what's better?

Ghee. Always ghee. There is nothing in the world that makes Indian food (and most food, to be honest) taste better than the rich, nutty flavor of ghee. You should be able to find ghee in most health food stores or Indian grocers, but if not, it's easy to make yourself: Melt a stick of butter over medium-low heat in a medium saucepan, turn the heat off, skim the white stuff off the top, and you'll be left with clear ghee!

All this said, I know that ghee isn't universally available. I tried each and every single one of these recipes with oil (mainly olive oil), and they turned out exceptionally. So, yes, ghee is great, but trust that you can go just as confidently with oil (or regular butter, when specified).

Speaking of oil, can I use types other than olive oil?

Yes! My mom and I have come to love the taste of olive oil in Indian cuisine, but other neutral oils like avocado oil and grapeseed oil will work just fine.

When a recipe says to adjust salt, how much is the right amount?

Salt is great! We love salt! But please take the salt measurements in this book with a grain of salt (pun intended). If you generally like things a little less or a little more salty, adjust accordingly.

Why should I trust you?

That is a great question. I am not a splashy TV personality or the chef of a big-name restaurant. So why trust in these recipes over those in any other cookbook? Well, first, there's my mom—the lady is so damn intuitive in the kitchen that I constantly found myself in awe of her ability to put flavors together in innovative but seamless ways when testing these recipes. This is not your grandma's cookbook: This is the food of a wildly sharp working mother who could put a healthy, composed, and delicious meal on the table in twenty minutes (without ever staining her white shirt) and then two days later host a twelve-course dinner party inspired by her latest trip to the Middle East, having cooked everything in a raw silk sari with no pins (for the non-Indians, this is a *feat*).

There's also the testing. Every single recipe in this book has been tested at least twice by me, edited by the fiercely talented recipe wizard Aralyn Beaumont, tested three more times by 100+ home cooks just like you, and in some cases re-edited and retested by my mother and me. I've put in the time to making these recipes as easy as possible, and THEY WORK. You have my word.

Can't I just use prepackaged curry powder/garam masala/ Trader Joe's tikka masala powder?

Listen, I'm not opposed to a spice blend every once in a while. But the answer is no—you cannot use any kind of prepackaged powder. Why? Because they are often made with old, stale spices and end up tasting like sawdust, and more important, the spice combos in these recipes are relatively straightforward. I'll never ask you to use twelve different spices in a single recipe, or make a bunch of very complicated spice blends. These are accessible recipes with a few essential spices. If you've been using packaged garam masala your whole life, you will be pleasantly shocked at how much more flavor comes from using whole spices, and how little effort these dishes actually require.

Should I seed my chiles?

I don't, and you shouldn't, either! Live a little!

What if I can't find one spice that the recipe calls for?

Use your best judgment. If the recipe calls for, like, a tablespoon of cumin and that's the only flavoring in the entire dish, you should probably go get the cumin or move along to another recipe. But if the recipe only calls for a small amount and there are four other spices—my mom's going to yell at me for saying this, but . . . I think it's perfectly fine to skip. There were a few instances during recipe testing when I accidentally omitted a spice, or swapped one spice for another. And it was all fiiiiine. Everything is fine. I'll tell you this over and over again in the book, but my mom's recipes are forgiving. You will end up with something delicious even if it's missing one tiny ingredient.

All that said, I've also included in-a-pinch substitutes in the chart on page 24, should you not be able to find a certain spice.

What do I serve all this food with?

I've made serving suggestions in the individual recipes, but if all else fails . . . rice and/or roti (or whole wheat tortillas), always. They're the best vehicles for sopping up all that delicious sauce!

Why are there no recipes for flan or eggplant in this cookbook?

Wow, those are oddly specific things! But they both happen to be my mom's least favorite dishes/ingredients in the entire world. So if you were hoping for a killer salted caramel flan or roasted eggplant dish, you're probably better off finding another cookbook.

Otherwise . . . onward!

Let's cook!

ESSENTIALS

How to Cook Rice

You should know how to make rice. In Indian cooking, rice is an auto accompaniment to most meals. My father is preprogrammed to stumble into the kitchen when he smells that dinner is almost ready, rinse some rice over the sink, and throw it in the microwave. Yes, we microwave our rice and it tastes great (but don't worry, I've included a stovetop version, too). Through the years, my mom has substituted "healthier" grains like quinoa and freekeh for rice. But everyone in the family can agree: There is nothing that goes better with a piping-hot bowl of dal or *sabzi* than snow-white, fluffy, long-grain basmati rice.

For those who own a multi-cooker (like an Instant Pot) or a rice cooker, rice is a cinch. But if you don't have one of those, here are our family's simple, tried-and-true cooking methods for long-grain rice.

**1 cup dry
=
~3 cups
cooked**

tip: Keep in mind that not every box/packet/bag of rice is the same, so be sure to check the back of the package for any specific cooking instructions.

In a microwave

1   Rinse the rice thoroughly in cold water.

2   Combine 1 cup rice and 2 cups water in a medium microwave-safe bowl and microwave on high for 16 to 20 minutes. (For ½ cup rice, reduce the water to 1 cup water and cook for 7 to 10 minutes.) Check on the rice halfway through, and if most of the water is gone, reduce the cook time. When the rice is done, all the water will have evaporated, and there should be grains sticking up on top like grass.

3   Fluff the rice with a fork and let rest for 10 minutes before serving.

On a stovetop

1   Rinse the rice thoroughly in cold water.

2   Combine 1 cup rice and 1½ cups water in a small pot or saucepan and bring the water to a gentle boil over medium-high heat. Turn the heat down to low, cover, and cook for 15 to 20 minutes. (For ½ cup rice, reduce the water to ¾ cup and cook for 10 to 15 minutes.)

3   Fluff the rice with a fork and let rest for 10 minutes before serving.

How to Cook White Quinoa

1 cup dry = ~3 cups cooked

As much as we adore rice, our family also possesses an unapologetic love for quinoa. We love the protein content, the nutty, chewy grains, and the way it soaks up the flavor of stews like a little caviar-shaped sponge. But far too often, quinoa ends up tasting like overly earthy rabbit food. I'm hopeful that the recipes in this book (specifically the Mushroom-Stuffed Mushrooms, page 99, and Quinoa Kheer, page 199) will change the minds of any quinoa skeptics, but the first step is knowing how to cook it properly—so it turns out fluffy, smooth, and without any bitter aftertaste.

note: These instructions apply to white quinoa (not the red stuff), which my mom has found to be the best accompaniment for Indian (and Indian-ish) food.

In a microwave

1   Put the quinoa in a fine-mesh strainer and rinse it thoroughly to remove the grain's natural bitter coating. This is important!

2   Combine 1 cup quinoa and 2½ cups water in a medium microwave-safe bowl and microwave on high for 20 to 23 minutes. (For ½ cup quinoa, reduce the water to 1¼ cups and cook for 10 to 13 minutes.) Check on the quinoa halfway through, and if most of the water is gone, reduce the cook time. When the quinoa is done, the water will have evaporated, the grains should be translucent, and the little white tails will have started sprouting.

3   Fluff the quinoa with a fork once and let rest for 10 minutes before serving.

On a stovetop

1   Put the quinoa in a fine-mesh strainer and rinse thoroughly to remove the grain's natural bitter coating.

2   Combine 1 cup quinoa and 2 cups water in a small pot or sauce-pan and bring the water to a boil over high heat. Lower the heat to medium, cover, and cook for 12 to 15 minutes, until the quinoa turns translucent and you can start to see their little white tails sprouting. (For ½ cup quinoa, reduce the water to 1 cup and cook for 8 to 12 minutes.)

3   Fluff the quinoa with a fork and let rest for 10 minutes before serving.

How to Boil Potatoes

Everyone always talks about the glorious char on *roasted* potatoes, or the oil-soaked greatness of *deep-fried* potatoes. Boiled potatoes don't get any love, when, in fact, they are the workhorses of the cooked potato family—they have a soft and silky interior, they soak into sauces nicely, and they are healthy but not bland! See what I mean in recipes like Aloo Ka Rasa (page 116), Aloo Paratha (page 145), and Dosa Potatoes (page 113). Learn how to boil a potato, and you can do ANYTHING! Well, maybe not *anything*, but you do then have the basis for a delicious soup/stew, an easy side (top 'em with the sauce of your choice!), or any lighter grain bowl or salad that's in need of a little heartiness and heft.

note: This recipe is for medium (5- to 6-ounce) russet potatoes, which are what you'll find most often in this book, but I've also noted adjusted cook times for baby potatoes.

In a microwave

1 Scrub the potatoes clean and pat dry.

2 Pierce each potato 5 times on each side with a fork. (No need to pierce baby red potatoes or new potatoes with a fork.)

3 Place the potatoes in a microwave-safe bowl, add a little bit of water to the bottom of the bowl, and microwave for 5 minutes on high. Remove (carefully!) from the microwave, flip the potatoes, and microwave for 5 minutes on high. (For baby red potatoes or new potatoes, microwave for 7 to 8 minutes—no need to flip.)

4 Let cool for 10 minutes. Once the potatoes are cool enough to handle, this is the best time to peel them, if the recipe calls for that.

On a stovetop

1 Place the potatoes in a small pot and add enough water to fully submerge them.

2 Bring the water to a boil over high heat, then reduce the heat to medium and cook for 20 to 25 minutes, until the potatoes can be very easily pierced with a fork. (For baby red potatoes or new potatoes, cook for 10 to 15 minutes.)

3 Drain, rinse with cold water, and let cool for 10 minutes. Once the potatoes are cool enough to handle, this is the best time to peel them, if the recipe calls for that.

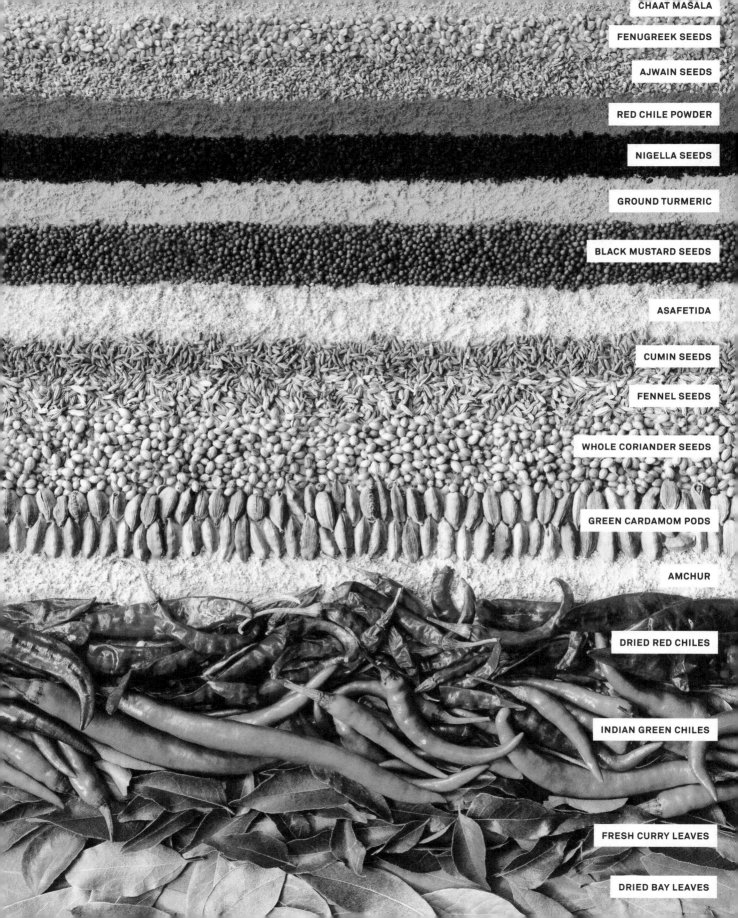

CHAAT MASALA

FENUGREEK SEEDS

AJWAIN SEEDS

RED CHILE POWDER

NIGELLA SEEDS

GROUND TURMERIC

BLACK MUSTARD SEEDS

ASAFETIDA

CUMIN SEEDS

FENNEL SEEDS

WHOLE CORIANDER SEEDS

GREEN CARDAMOM PODS

AMCHUR

DRIED RED CHILES

INDIAN GREEN CHILES

FRESH CURRY LEAVES

DRIED BAY LEAVES

Fantastic Spices and Lentils (and Where to Find Them)

Here's a peek at some of the spices and lentils you might find in the Krishna family pantry. Yes, it seems like a lot. No, you don't have to buy them all. Please don't slam the book closed and run far, far away. I just wanted to lay everything out in one convenient place.

The thing that annoys me about cookbooks is how they ask you to buy all these pantry items to use in *one* recipe, and then those ingredients end up collecting dust in the back of your cabinet. Also, the number one question I got from folks testing these recipes was, **"WHERE DO I BUY THIS?"** The short answer: Overall, Amazon or health food stores are your best friends for spices and lentils, but try to support your local Indian grocery store if you have one.

So I put together this comprehensive chart of all the different kinds of spices and lentils that my family loves, *plus* how you can use them beyond just the recipes in this book, and—if ALL ELSE FAILS and you've got to push the emergency button—some suggested substitutes (spoiler alert: My mom has taught me that cumin seeds are apparently a replacement for everything). One other thing: Whenever possible, try to buy the spices in their whole form—not ground. Whole spices make all the difference in terms of flavor.

As for lentils, there are loads of varieties, but here are the family favorites you'll find in this book. A kind of confusing thing about the names of these? The color in the name doesn't always correspond to the actual color of the lentil. For example, whole red lentils are actually brown in color! (I think the naming is because the skin is brown, while the inside is red.) Who knew?! At the health food stores I've been to, the names/colors *seem* to be more closely aligned because they are simply named for the exterior color, but if you're at an Indian grocery store, don't get tricked!!!

SPICE GUIDE

SPICE	ALSO KNOWN AS	WHAT'S THE FLAVOR?	WHERE DO I FIND IT?
Ajwain Seeds	Bishop's weed, carom	Sharp, bitter, and oregano-like—an acquired but utterly delightful taste	Indian grocery stores or Amazon
Amchur	Dried mango powder	Fruity, tangy	Indian grocery stores or Amazon
Asafetida	Hing	Oniony, pungent, MSG-like	Indian grocery stores or Amazon
Black Mustard Seeds	n/a	Bitter, earthy	Indian grocery stores, Amazon, and some health food stores
Chaat Masala	n/a	Funky, salty	Indian grocery stores or Amazon
Cumin Seeds	Jeera	Warm, nutty, smoky	Most commercial grocery stores

HOW DO I USE IT?	IN-A-PINCH SUBSTITUTE
The most classic pairing is ajwain and okra, which you'll find in **Bhindi (page 76)**. I like to use it with sweeter and milder-tasting vegetables that mellow out its sharpness, like in the corn-and-carrot-heavy grain bowl **Dalia (page 169)**, or the tempura-esque **Chickpea Flour Green Beans (page 90)**.	Cumin seeds
Use it in any dish where you want to add a funky sweet-and-sour component, like **Bhindi (page 76)**. It's fantastic in marinades for chicken and fish, like in **Garlic-Ginger Chicken with Cilantro and Mint (page 187)**. If a dish needs acid, but you don't have limes or lemons, throw in some amchur!	Lime juice
Think of asafetida like a super booster that harmoniously unites and enhances the flavors of all the other spices in a dish. Make sure to toast it in oil or butter to mellow out its funk. Then mix it with any combination of cumin, mustard seeds, garlic, ginger, or other common Indian spices (it's best when paired with other things). It's excellent atop a lentil stew (**Priya's Dal, page 152**), sautéed vegetables (**Kaddu, page 115**), or any other gravy-based dish (**Spinach and Feta Cooked Like Paneer, page 83**).	Garlic powder (a very imperfect substitute)
These are often toasted in oil along with fresh curry leaves, and together they add crunch and a piquant bite to any dish—try the combo with plain rice, soft veggies like **Dosa Potatoes (page 113)** or **South Indian–ish Squash (page 94)**, or as a topper for lime-y salads, like **Mustard Seed and Curry Leaf Carrot Salad (page 105)**.	Brown mustard seeds (not yellow/white mustard seeds) or cumin seeds
A combination of spices, and an instant flavor-enhancer that tastes good on essentially everything. It's particularly great on potatoes, like **Indian-ish Baked Potatoes (page 119)**; paired with sharp cheese, as in **Tomato-Cheese Masala Toast (page 126)**; and, surprisingly, atop almond butter in **Chaat Masala–Almond Butter Toast (page 122)**. You can also sprinkle it atop sautés and stews to add depth, or use it as a savory topping for fresh or grilled fruit.	n/a (Sorry, there's just no substitute for the magic of chaat masala.)
The building block for so many North Indian dishes—particularly vegetable dishes. Heat oil, throw in some cumin seeds, and you've got the basis for **Roasted Aloo Gobhi (page 96)**; **Red Pepper, Potato, and Peanut Sabzi (page 93)**; or **Caramelized Ginger Mushrooms (page 104)**. A common ingredient in a chhonk—tempered spices sprinkled atop stews like **Priya's Dal (page 152)** or **Khichdi (page 158)** to add flavor and richness. Also great in a marinade for steak, chicken, or lamb; a bean stew; a spicy noodle dish; or any kind of fried rice.	Caraway seeds

SPICE	ALSO KNOWN AS	WHAT'S THE FLAVOR?	WHERE DO I FIND IT?
Dried Bay Leaves	Bay laurel	Mild, aromatic, fresh	Any commercial grocery store
Dried Red Chiles	Lots of things! Dried Thai chiles, dried Kashmiri chiles, and dried chile de árbol all work great. Don't sweat about varietals.	Pungent, fiery	Any commercial grocery store
Fennel Seeds	Saunf	Sweet, licorice-like	Most commercial grocery stores, Amazon, or Indian grocery stores
Fenugreek Seeds	Methi	Nutty, earthy	Health food stores, Amazon, Indian grocery stores
Fresh Curry Leaves	Sweet neem leaves, kadhi patta	Fresh, aromatic, slightly tangy	Indian grocery stores, Amazon
Green Cardamom Pods	n/a	Sweet, herbaceous	Health food stores, Amazon, Indian grocery stores

HOW DO I USE IT?	IN-A-PINCH SUBSTITUTE
The subtle flavor is best brought out when added to hearty stews like **Aloo Ka Rasa (page 116)**, and rice dishes like **Khichdi (page 158)**. It's particularly great in meat stews and chili, where it cuts through that richness.	n/a
In Indian cuisine, red chiles are typically used in a chhonk (see page 32), like **Priya's Dal (page 152)** and **Kadhi (page 157)**. Dried red chiles can also be blended with warm spices like cumin and cinnamon and used as a rub for meats, or rehydrated and pureed into a sauce that can be thrown into salad dressings or dips, or used on roasted vegetables.	Most any kind of dried chiles will work, except for ones with a distinctly smoky flavor, like chipotle chiles. You can also use fresh red chiles as a last resort, but slit them in half before you use them to prevent splattering.
Fennel seeds nicely complement any dish made with okra or bell peppers. They work well as an aromatic dry rub for barbecue, as a flavoring for sausage, or in any other kind of ground meat–based sauce. In Indian cuisine, fennel seeds are also munched on whole as a natural breath-freshener.	Aniseeds
It's best to toast the seeds in a pan (either dry or with some oil) to bring out their aroma. Then they are often used to offset sweetness in sautéed vegetables or stews, in dishes like **Kaddu (page 115)** and **Shortcut Chhole (page 153)**. You can also add them to any spice blend—say, a dry rub for meat, or a seasoning for lentils or beans—that needs a little balance and intrigue.	Yellow mustard seeds
See Black Mustard Seeds.	Lime leaves
In savory cooking, either use them whole (but crushed), or remove the seeds from the pods and crush them into a powder. Cardamom adds a pleasant aroma and a slight sweetness to any kind of tomato-based gravy or sauce, like in **Matar Paneer (page 70)**. It's also a fragrant flavoring for dairy-based desserts, like **Shrikhand (page 196)** or **Shahi Toast (page 200)**. It can be used to amp up a cup of tea, like **Cardamom Chai (page 210)**, or the pods can be munched on whole as a natural breath-freshener.	Ground cardamom (in this book, if a recipe calls for ground cardamom, freshly ground is always best)

SPICE	ALSO KNOWN AS	WHAT'S THE FLAVOR?	WHERE DO I FIND IT?
Ground Turmeric	n/a	Earthy, bitter	Most commercial grocery stores
Indian Green Chiles	Lots of things! Serranos, Thai chiles, or really any kind of slender green chiles you find at the Indian grocery store work great.	Fruity, hot	Any commercial grocery store **** Use kitchen scissors to mince fresh chiles to prevent getting any of the spicy juices on your fingers**
Nigella Seeds	Black onion seeds	Bitter, nutty	Most commercial grocery stores, Amazon, or Indian grocery stores
Red Chile Powder	Lots of things! Kashmiri red chile powder, cayenne, and hot paprika all work great for these recipes. Don't sweat about varietals. However, this is not the same thing as "chili powder," the spice blend used to make chili.	If it hasn't been sitting in your cabinet for years, fiery and intense. Just make sure to taste your red chile powder before using it, as some are spicier than others.	Any commercial grocery store
Whole Coriander Seeds	Cilantro seeds	Nutty, sweet, citrus-like	Health food stores, Amazon, Indian grocery stores

Turmeric is what gives many Indian dishes their distinct color and earthy depths, but it needs to be cooked to activate its flavors and health benefits. In savory cooking, it should be sautéed in oil before being added to the vegetables/meats/rice/etc. When using turmeric in drinks (ahem: turmeric lattes), make sure it's heated up with the milk, not just mixed in at the end.	n/a **** To get turmeric stains out of your dishes, use a combination of hot water and distilled white vinegar; for clothes, sqeeze a generous amount of lemon juice on top of the stain and then wash as normal.**
Minced green chiles are a way to add both freshness and heat to any dish, whether it's a salad like **Kachumber (page 107)**, a sauce like **Cilantro Chutney (page 62)**, a stew like **Aloo Ka Rasa (page 116)**, or a grain dish like **Quinoa Shrimp Pulao (page 174)**.	Any fruity green chile with a good amount of spice. Don't sweat about varietals, but do give 'em a nibble before you add them, because green chiles vary in heat.
Nigella seeds are great when sautéed in oil alongside other seeds like mustard, cumin, fenugreek, and fennel. This fried multiseed combo can be used as a topping for a fresh salad, like **Green Chile and Cherry Tomato Pickle (page 64)**, or a component in a sauce like **Mango Launji (page 66)**. Nigella seeds are also excellent in any kind of potato dish.	Cumin seeds or celery seeds
Anything and everything that needs a dash of heat.	Really, anything red and spicy and not smoky (so stay away from things like guajillo chile powder)
Typically used in their freshly ground form, in Indian cuisine, they add warmth and nuttiness to sauces like the ones in **Spinach and Feta Cooked Like Saag Paneer (page 83)** or **Matar Paneer (page 70)**. They are a nice aromatic component in rice dishes, marinades for meat—like in **Garlic-Ginger Chicken with Cilantro and Mint (page 187)**—or any kind of pickled vegetable. To maximize their aroma, toast them dry before adding them to a sauce or marinade.	Ground coriander (though if a recipe calls for ground coriander, freshly ground is always best), NOT fresh coriander

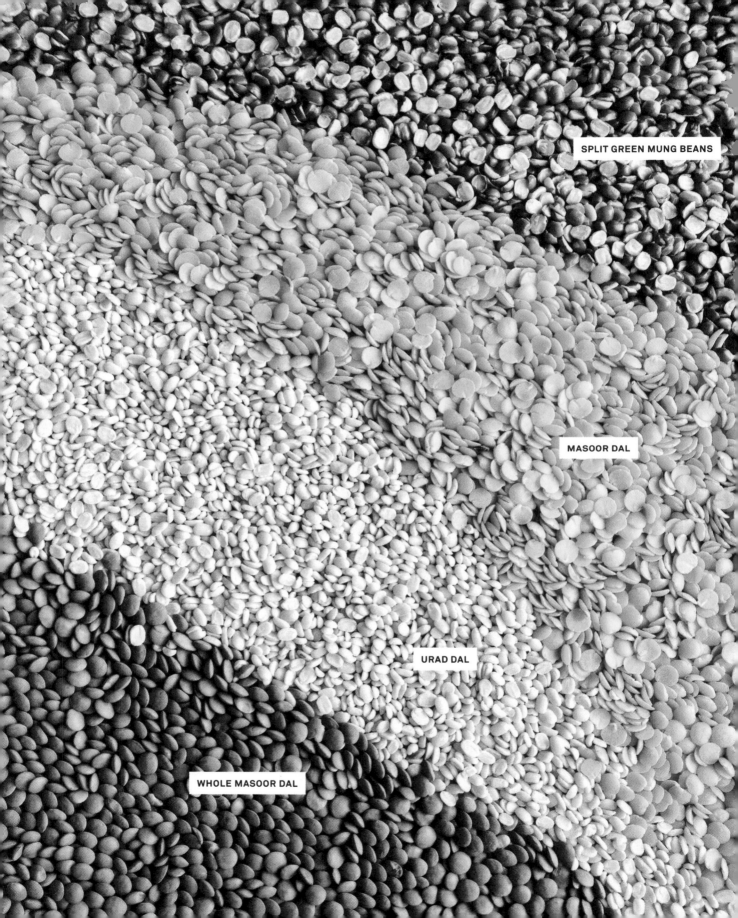

SPLIT GREEN MUNG BEANS

MASOOR DAL

URAD DAL

WHOLE MASOOR DAL

LENTIL GUIDE

TIP: Always rinse your lentils. This will remove any unwanted debris and dirt.

LENTIL	ALSO KNOWN AS	WHAT ARE THEY LIKE?	WHERE DO I FIND THEM?	OTHER USES BESIDES STEWS
Split Green Mung Beans	n/a	Tiny, easy to digest	Health food stores, Amazon, Indian grocery stores	Mix them with rice and make Khichdi (page 158), or mix them into a salad to add some heft.
Masoor Dal	Red lentils, split and dehusked pink lentils (not to be confused with whole masoor dal, or whole red lentils; this variety is pinkish-orange in color)	Smooth, soupy, quick-cooking	Health food stores, Amazon, Indian grocery stores	Use as a thickening agent in a broth or dip.
Urad Dal	Ivory-white lentils, split and dehusked black gram lentils (but they are white in color)	Skinny, chewy, risotto-like	Amazon, Indian grocery stores	Sauté cooked urad dal with some olive oil, garlic, and herbs for a healthy-ish lentil salad that *almost* feels like you're eating pasta or rice.
Whole Masoor Dal	Kali masoor dal, sabut masoor dal, brown lentils, whole red lentils (not to be confused with red lentils; these are brown in color)	Chubby, buttery (my personal favorite)	Health food stores, Amazon, Indian grocery stores	Salads! These lentils hold their shape well and absorb dressings nicely.

On Chhonk, the Greatest Indian Cooking Technique Ever

There are going to be many times in this book where a recipe will instruct you to separately heat up some ghee or oil in a little pan or butter warmer, throw in some spices, and then pour that mixture over a finished dish. This will often be in addition to the spices you have already added to the dish, which may prompt you to ask, "Why do I need to dirty another pan? Why do I have to separately toast these spices in oil? Why can't I just put them in the dish with the rest of the spices?"

Allow me to introduce you to the most revelatory Indian cooking technique ever: chhonk, also known as tempering or tadka. If you take nothing else away from this book, remember the magic of chhonk. When you temper spices in oil, you not only bring out the aromas and the intensity of the spices, but you end up with this complex infused oil that adds instant richness and depth to any sort of dish, whether it's a dal or a sabzi or paneer.

Start with boiled potatoes, sautéed greens, a plain ol' bowl of grains . . . add salt, then pour chhonk over the top. That's all you need. Pour chhonk over nachos! Noodles! Steak! Literally anything that needs a flavor blast of any kind.

There are two kinds of chhonk you'll find in this book: one is a spicy, nutty red-chile-and-cumin-based version (inspired by North Indian cooking), and the other is a bright, earthy curry-leaf-and-mustard-seed-based version (taken from South Indian cooking). Here's a handy chart to help you incorporate chhonk into your everyday cooking.

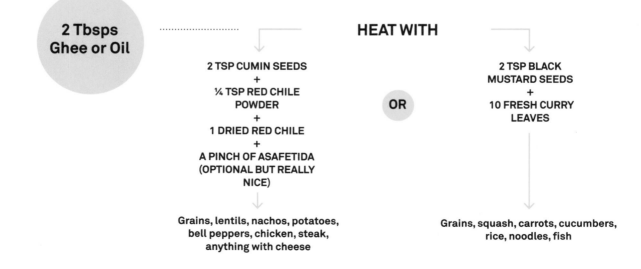

2 Tbsps Ghee or Oil

HEAT WITH

2 TSP CUMIN SEEDS
+
¼ TSP RED CHILE POWDER
+
1 DRIED RED CHILE
+
A PINCH OF ASAFETIDA (OPTIONAL BUT REALLY NICE)

OR

2 TSP BLACK MUSTARD SEEDS
+
10 FRESH CURRY LEAVES

Grains, lentils, nachos, potatoes, bell peppers, chicken, steak, anything with cheese

Grains, squash, carrots, cucumbers, rice, noodles, fish

A Few of Our Favorite Things

(The Krishna Family's Kitchen Mainstays That Are Not Spices or Lentils)

Smucker's Strawberry Preserves

We've tried all the fancy artisanal jams on the planet, and we keep coming back to the good old grocery store Smucker's Strawberry Preserves. Like Heinz ketchup or Martin's potato rolls, Smucker's preserves are perfect in their nostalgic simplicity. The texture is pleasantly but not alarmingly bouncy, with little chunks of strawberries in every bite. The tart-to-sweet ratio is spot on. And I love the jar with the red-and-white-checkered lid. We eat this stuff by itself, mixed with plain yogurt, or in my favorite sandwich of all time: the PB&J.

Haldiram's Bikaneri Bhujia

Imagine your favorite chip but in pourable, sprinkle-shaped, spicy form, and you've got bikaneri bhujia—fried noodle-like bits made of chickpea flour and spices. These little snacks are everything—crispy, salty, creepingly hot, I-want-to-upturn-this-entire-bag-into-my-mouth goodness. We eat bhujia straight out of the bag, as a crunchy topping for any kind of sabzi or starch (like Sabudana, page 182, or Chile Peanut Rice, page 168), and atop buttered toast. We want to bathe in bikaneri bhujia. In fact, we actively try not to have too much of it around at any time, because no member of the Krishna family can resist the siren call of these tiny, crispy treats.

Dispense-Your-Own Almond Butter from Whole Foods

As Texans, as far as health food grocers go, we are loyalists to the beloved Lone Star State mainstay, Central Market. But the one thing Whole Foods has that Central Market does not is that delightful machine that grinds almonds into silky-soft unsalted almond butter. It's really fun to use, and there's no nut butter better than fresh nut butter.

Lijjat Punjabi Masala Papad

Papad, or papadum, are thin, crisp crackers made of lentils, designed for munching alongside any and all Indian stews. What I love about this particular variety is that they are studded with black pepper, and if this does not become clear from reading this book, the Krishnas freaking love black pepper. For all the health nuts out there, papad are toasted

or baked, not fried—so you've got all the addictiveness of a chip without any of the bad stuff. My parents are known to snack on papad with a cold Texas beer (preferably a Shiner).

Shatila Baklava

I have written many love letters to the baklava from Shatila, a Middle Eastern bakery in Detroit, on various corners of the Internet, and the gist of them all is this: This is the best baklava in America—buttery, honey-laced treasures made with grade-A nuts that inspire a manic devotion in my family. We used to have to wait for our Michigan cousins to visit us to get our hands on this baklava. Thankfully, the store just relaunched its e-commerce site. Bless.

Explore Cuisine Organic Edamame Spaghetti

This discovery was thanks to my mom's friend Durrain, who does product tastings at Costco for a living. She gave my mom a box, and we were immediately impressed by its delicate yet al dente texture, ability to cling to sauces, and crazy-high protein and fiber content. Eat a bowl of edamame spaghetti, and be prepared to *really* have to go. But it will be the most satisfying dump you've ever taken, and that, as my dad would say, is worth its weight in gold!

Ritu's Overly Generalized Guide to Making the Indian Food in This Book

One day, fed up with all my questions about her cooking, my mom grabbed a piece of paper and drew up a chart to illustrate how she generally thinks about pairing ingredients and flavors in the Indian food she makes. My mind was blown. Here's that diagram she drew in full—may it help you to make Indian cooking an everyday, on-the-fly thing!

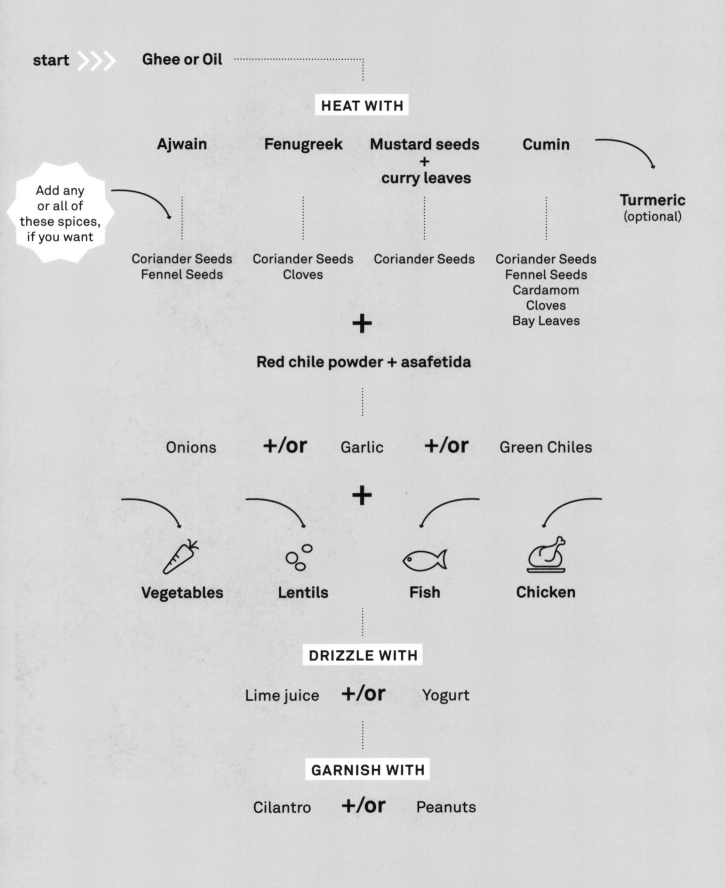

start >>> **Ghee or Oil**

HEAT WITH

Ajwain **Fenugreek** **Mustard seeds + curry leaves** **Cumin**

Turmeric (optional)

Add any or all of these spices, if you want

Coriander Seeds	Coriander Seeds	Coriander Seeds	Coriander Seeds
Fennel Seeds	Cloves		Fennel Seeds
			Cardamom
			Cloves
			Bay Leaves

+

Red chile powder + asafetida

Onions **+/or** Garlic **+/or** Green Chiles

+

Vegetables **Lentils** **Fish** **Chicken**

DRIZZLE WITH

Lime juice **+/or** Yogurt

GARNISH WITH

Cilantro **+/or** Peanuts

Ritu's Tips for Hosting and Living Graciously

Taste every dish for lime and salt.

Never underestimate the power of a statement necklace—and statement earrings to go with the statement necklace.

Change out of your work clothes as soon as you get home. You'll immediately feel more relaxed.

Always take the stairs if you can.

Appetizers are overrated, and distract from all the hard work you put into a meal.

Two and a half inches are as high a heel as you'll ever need. Anything taller is a recipe for bunions.

Use cloth napkins, even if you're using paper plates. They make everything look better.

Better to be overdressed than to be underdressed.

Invest in nice pottery. It will make your food look ten times more impressive.

For dinner parties, try to be done cooking food at least two hours before guests come over, so you can have a pre-party glass of wine.

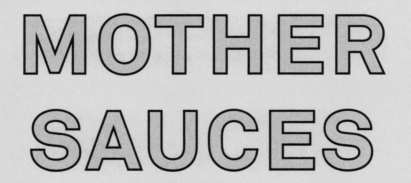

MOTHER
SAUCES

Ginger-Lime Strips

Makes ¼ cup (can be very easily multiplied)

——

One 3-inch piece fresh ginger, peeled and julienned (see Tip)

¼ teaspoon kosher salt

¼ cup lime juice (from about 2 limes)

This little jar of ginger and lime—a sort of quick pickle that was a staple in my mom's home growing up—will change your life. Whenever I make a stew, stir-fry, soup—literally anything hot and/or hearty that needs a little zing—I throw in a few of these ginger-lime strips as a flavorful garnish. For any recipe that calls for ginger, you can use these limey ginger bits for an extra shot of brightness or vice-versa: Pour the ginger-infused lime juice on any dish where you would typically add lime. It's also a great use for those empty sauce or jam jars we all inexplicably hoard. For those who like it hot, do as my dad does and throw a few chopped green chiles into the mix.

1   Place the ginger in a 2-ounce glass jar. Add the salt, close the lid, and shake to mix. Add the lime juice, cover, and refrigerate for at least 3 hours before using. This condiment keeps, refrigerated, for up to 2 weeks.

> **tip:** The easiest way to julienne ginger is to cut the piece of ginger in half lengthwise, cut it into slices, also lengthwise, then cut each slice into thin strips. Cut with, not against, the grain (you know you're going against the grain if you see tiny threads coming out of the ginger as you cut it).

Dad's Yogurt

Makes 1 quart

―――

4 cups organic whole milk

¼ cup full-fat plain yogurt (see Note)

I could probably write a separate book on my dad's yogurt. Actually, my dad should probably write that book, because the guy knows more about coagulated milk solids than any human ever should. He's been making yogurt for decades, using a yogurt culture that's over thirty years old (you can freeze leftover yogurt and use it many moons later as a culture). And though cooking websites may tell you that you need special machines and containers to make yogurt, all you really need are a sturdy pot and a clean index finger (more on that soon). And the coolest part about homemade yogurt is how it evolves and improves over time, since you can use one batch of yogurt as the culture for the next one. Your first batch will taste pretty much exactly like the first yogurt culture you use. But your fifth batch may turn out even richer, creamier, and tangier. My dad's yogurt culture is essentially his third child, who he has raised to be smooth, slightly sweet, and pleasantly chunky. It never talks back or complains about the fact that he drives too slowly. You, too, can raise a yogurt child of your own! You'll never go back to the store-bought stuff again.

note: Choose your favorite brand of yogurt, as that's essentially what you'll be replicating—just make sure it has active cultures as an ingredient.

1   Evenly coat the bottom of a medium Dutch oven or other heavy-bottomed pot with a thin layer of water (this will prevent the milk from sticking to the bottom of the pot). Set the pot over high heat and add the milk. Heat the milk until it just comes to a boil, watching it closely—*as soon* as you start to see bubbles forming, take the pot off the heat. Let the milk cool until it reaches 130°F, 30 to 35 minutes. If you don't have a thermometer, the milk should be warm enough that you can comfortably stick your (clean!) finger into it—it should feel hot, but not so hot as to scald your finger (think of a Jacuzzi).

2   While the milk is cooling, smear the bottom of a 1-quart container with 1 teaspoon of the yogurt.

3   When the milk has cooled, add the rest of the yogurt to the milk and stir with a whisk or small spoon for 3 minutes to make sure the yogurt has completely dissolved into the milk.

continued

Dad's Yogurt, continued

4   Pour the milk-yogurt mixture into the container and loosely cover the top, leaving a little room for air to get out.

5   Place the container inside an unheated oven with the oven light on and let sit for 2½ hours (see Tip). Check the yogurt: When it is done, it will be set (not liquid) but still jiggle like Jell-O. If it's not yet set, leave it in the oven for 1 hour more. Depending on the temperature and humidity outside, the setting process could take up to 5½ hours, so don't fret if it's not done the first time you check it. When the yogurt is done, place it in the fridge to chill and fully set overnight before using. The yogurt will keep, covered, for 4 to 6 weeks (it'll start to get pretty sour after 2 weeks, which, depending on your tastes, could be a good or bad thing).

tip: Depending on the temperature outside, you may want to vary the conditions a bit. In the winter, we leave the oven light on the entire time it takes for the yogurt to set; in the warmer months, we shut the light off about an hour after we place the yogurt into the oven.

tip: Want Greek-style yogurt? Line a colander with cheesecloth or overlapping coffee filters and set it over a bowl or deep plate. Pour in the finished yogurt and refrigerate overnight to allow the whey to drain out and the yogurt to thicken.

Why My Yogurt Is Fabulous

By Shailendra Krishna

I grew up with homemade yogurt every day. In Indian cuisine, yogurt is essential. In the north, we tend to have it at the end of every meal—it's a way of balancing out all the spices. And I suspect the probiotics also regulate our systems, if you know what I mean.

When Ritu and I came to America in 1980, all we could get was really crappy yogurt. And then one day, I tasted homemade yogurt at a friend's place in Massachusetts, and it was great. I asked for a recipe, and the first time I made it, it was so damn good that I decided I would be the one to make the yogurt.

At first, yogurt was a hit-or-miss affair. Sometimes it would set, sometimes it wouldn't. And then Ritu's mom came here, observed me making it, and made a few suggestions that really changed how I do things. First, when I'd pour the culture into the warm milk, I used to just let it sit, but she told me that you want to *really* mix the culture into the warm milk—that's what ensures it will set. Second, she told me that the ideal way to test the temperature of the milk when it's in the pot is to stick your clean finger into it: If it feels slightly uncomfortable but not scalding, it is the right temperature. We didn't really do thermometers.

What makes my yogurt good is the refinement over time. Every time I make yogurt, I will mix some of the milk with the culture in a small cup and set it aside. That is my seed for the next batch. I started with generation zero—now I am probably on generation 30,000. Today, the culture that I have is superior to earlier versions—it creates yogurt that sets quickly (in two and a half to three hours versus a decade ago, when it would take six hours); is nice and sweet; and is firm, not stringy. It is just perfect.

Making yogurt has become my ritual. When I come back from a walk, or if I want to take my mind off work, I will take a break and make yogurt. It is very relaxing and fulfilling. It is also the one thing Mom will never touch. It is my domain. I love that when Meera and Priya come home, I have to make an extra batch because they like it so much. I have given away my culture to so many people so that they can make their own at home. I have reduced this process down to a repeatable algorithm. That's how I like to do things.

My yogurt is fabulous. I have a cup a day. It keeps my system nice and regular. What more could you want?

Clockwise from top: Squash Raita, Basic Raita, Cucumber Raita, Mustard Seed and Curry Leaf Raita, and Potato Raita

Raita

Raita is the cooling foil to just about every Indian dish. It's the fire hose that extinguishes your tongue when you accidentally bite into that whole chile (the fact that Indians choose to put whole chiles into dishes at all just seems like a cruel, cruel joke to me). Raita is also endlessly versatile. Simultaneously sweet, salty, and tangy, it can be eaten by itself, kind of like a savory side, or used as a sauce for drizzling over grilled chicken or fish. Here are five of my mom's best variations on raita, starting with the most basic—the standard sweet 'n' spicy yogurt sauce—and ending with my personal favorite, a raita punctuated by squishy, mellow dollops of squash and freshly toasted cumin. There are also two South Indian–inspired raitas (my dad's personal favorites), bedazzled with earthy mustard seeds and curry leaves for crunch. Plus an *extremely* refreshing grated cucumber raita.

tip: These raitas keep in the fridge for up to 3 days, but are best eaten fresh!

BASIC RAITA

Serves 4

2 cups full-fat plain yogurt
¾ teaspoon kosher salt
1 tablespoon granulated sugar
½ teaspoon red chile powder

1 Combine all the ingredients in a small bowl and mix well.

SQUASH RAITA

Serves 4

1 cup diced (½-inch pieces) peeled butternut or acorn squash (about a quarter of a small squash)

1 recipe Basic Raita (above)

1 tablespoon ground cumin (freshly ground is best)

1 small Indian green chile or serrano chile, finely chopped

¼ cup chopped fresh cilantro (stems and leaves), for garnish

1 Combine the squash and 1 cup water in a small pot and bring the water to a boil over high heat. Reduce the heat to medium-low, cover, and cook for 15 to 20 minutes, until the squash is fork-tender. (Alternatively, put the squash in a small microwave-safe bowl, add a ¼-inch layer of water, and microwave on high for 6 to 7 minutes, until the squash is fork-tender.) Drain and let cool for 10 to 15 minutes. Transfer the cooled squash to a medium bowl and stir in the basic raita.

2 In a small pan over low heat, toast the cumin, stirring occasionally, until it is fragrant and turns a shade darker, 3 to 4 minutes. Add the cumin and chile to the squash raita, mix well, and garnish with the cilantro.

CUCUMBER RAITA

Serves 4

1 Persian cucumber or half an English cucumber, grated

1 recipe Basic Raita (page 49)

1 tablespoon ground cumin (freshly ground is best)

¼ cup chopped fresh cilantro (stems and leaves), for garnish

1   In a medium bowl, mix together the grated cucumber and the basic raita until well combined. Set aside.

2   In a small pan over low heat, toast the cumin, stirring occasionally, until it is fragrant and turns a shade darker, 3 to 4 minutes. Add the cumin to the cucumber raita, mix well, and garnish with the cilantro.

MUSTARD SEED AND CURRY LEAF RAITA

Serves 4

1 recipe Basic Raita (page 49)

2 tablespoons olive oil

1 tablespoon black mustard seeds

10 large fresh curry leaves, each leaf torn in half

1   Put the basic raita in a medium bowl and set aside.

2   In a small pan over medium-high heat, warm the oil. Once the oil begins to shimmer, add the black mustard seeds, and as soon as they begin to pop and dance around in the oil, which should be within seconds, remove the pan from the heat. Add the curry leaves, making sure they get fully coated in the oil (there may be more popping and splattering, and that's okay!). The leaves should immediately crisp up in the residual heat.

3   Gently combine the oil mixture (no need to let it cool) with the raita.

POTATO RAITA

Serves 4

2 small russet potatoes, boiled (see page 20) and cooled

1 recipe Mustard Seed and Curry Leaf Raita (above)

1   Peel the cooled potatoes and use your hands to break them into bite-size pieces. Put the Mustard Seed and Curry Leaf Raita in a medium bowl and fold in the potato pieces.

Spicy Olive Tapenade

Makes 1½ cups

———

1 cup pitted black olives, drained

½ cup pitted kalamata olives, drained

4 garlic cloves, crushed

1 tablespoon capers, drained

1½ teaspoons red chile flakes

¼ cup olive oil

Let me start by saying I love this olive tapenade so much that, in middle school, the dip inspired me to write a short story for English class called "Olive Tapenade" about a chic lady sitting in a park who falls in love with a janitor over . . . you guessed it . . . hummus (kidding—obviously it was olive tapenade). My mom started making this dip before she even knew that olive tapenade was a thing. Our family just really liked olives, so it made sense for her to blitz them into a briny, supercharged dip for us to eat with crackers, raw veggies, or toast. Ours is very unlike the traditional French tapenade—it nixes the anchovies (I've tried many times, and I just . . . can't), and ups the spice level with red chile flakes. There's also a very healthy amount of garlic in here because, well, garlic.

1 In a blender, combine all the ingredients and blend on low speed until chunky but not pasty. Transfer to a serving bowl. This dip keeps, refrigerated in an airtight container, for up to 2 weeks.

Lima Bean and Basil Dip

This dip combines the best parts of a pesto and a hummus—it's got the light, herbaceous quality of the former, and the creamy brightness of the latter. It's a winning match for sandwiches, crackers, and grain-based salads—and, like many of my mom's best culinary inventions, it was created by accident. Back in 2005, when she was going through her edamame phase (didn't we all?!), she was scrambling to make an edamame dip before company came over and realized that she was fresh out of the beans. An old, icy packet of neglected frozen lima beans was unearthed from the freezer, and we've never looked at lima beans the same since.

Makes about 1¼ cups

———

10 ounces frozen or cooked lima beans (1¼ cups)

8 large fresh basil leaves

1 teaspoon kosher salt, plus more if needed

1 teaspoon freshly ground black pepper

1 garlic clove, crushed

½ cup olive oil, plus more if needed

1 tablespoon fresh lime juice (from about half a lime), plus more if needed

1 If using frozen lima beans, put them in a microwave-safe dish and microwave for 5 minutes, until all the beans are thawed and warmed. Let cool to room temperature.

2 Transfer the lima beans to a blender, add the remaining ingredients, and blend to a chunky, hummus-like consistency. Scrape down the sides of the blender a few times to make sure the dip is uniformly blended. If the mixture is too thick to blend, add a few drops of olive oil to get it going.

3 Taste and adjust the lime juice and/or salt, if needed. Transfer to a serving bowl. This dip keeps, refrigerated in an airtight container, for up to 1 week.

Clockwise from top: Lima Bean and Basil Dip; Sun-Dried Tomato, Chile, and Garlic Dip (page 54); Sabudana (page 182); Tofu-Basil Endive Leaves (page 103); and Spicy Chickpea Dip (page 58)

Sun-Dried Tomato, Chile, and Garlic Dip

Remember sun-dried tomatoes? The '90s it-ingredient that was all the rage on restaurant menus and grocery aisles, then suddenly disappeared? What happened to it? Where did it go? I will never understand this, because sun-dried tomatoes, I firmly believe, are a perfect ingredient. They are salty and intense, delivering more umami in a single bite than any other non-cheese ingredient I can think of. They're like a Fruit Roll-Up version of a tomato, with all the fruit's best qualities turned way, way up. This is my mother's ode to one of my favorite things, in the form of a sweetish, briny, spiced-up dip that will fondly remind all your party guests about the partially opened container of sun-dried tomatoes they have sitting in the back of their fridge or pantry. Don't call it a comeback.

Makes 2 cups

1 cup sun-dried tomatoes (the dry kind, *not* the kind packed in oil)

1 garlic clove, crushed

1 teaspoon red chile flakes

1 tablespoon pitted kalamata olives, drained

1 tablespoon capers, drained

½ cup olive oil

½ teaspoon kosher salt

tip: This dip makes a great substitute for tomato sauce as a pizza base!

1   In a small bowl, soak the sun-dried tomatoes in 1 cup water for 2 hours. Drain the tomatoes, reserving the water.

2   In a food processor, combine the drained sun-dried tomatoes, garlic, red chile flakes, olives, capers, and olive oil and blend into a chunky, pesto-like dip. If the mixture isn't blending well, add some of the reserved tomato-soaking water a few drops at a time to get it going, making sure the dip stays thick and chunky.

3   Transfer the dip to a serving bowl and stir in the salt. This dip keeps, refrigerated in an airtight container, for up to 2 weeks.

Lime, Chile, and Garlic Dressing

Makes ¼ cup (can be easily multiplied)

────

¼ cup fresh lime juice (from about 2 limes)

1 small Indian green chile or serrano chile, finely chopped

1 teaspoon kosher salt

1 teaspoon granulated sugar

1 garlic clove, minced

Everyone has a go-to dressing—a put-this-on-any-assemblage-of-vegetables-and-it-will-taste-good secret weapon. This is my family's. It's essentially just lime juice supported by a few other balancing components—refreshing and light, with a sweet-salty edge. It's also similar to the base dressing for my mom's Kachumber (page 107), our most standard Indian salad, and it's perfect atop any kind of chopped salad. People are always surprised that there is no fat, like oil or mayo, in the dressing, but trust me: This is flavorful and robust enough on its own—like the tangy, tasty juice that pools on the bottom of a bowl of ceviche.

1   Combine all the ingredients in a small bowl and mix well. This dressing keeps, refrigerated in an airtight container, for just about a day, so best to finish it off quickly.

Black Pepper and Chile Baked Goat Cheese

In Houston, there is this restaurant my family loves called Star Pizza, introduced to us by my dad's brother. I love it because its creaky, homey former facade used to remind me of the Burrow (aka the Weasleys' house in Harry Potter). The pizza here is . . . fine. The appetizers are the reason you go. It's here where my mom and I discovered that the only thing better than plain goat cheese is spicy, bubbly, peppery, warm goat cheese. With that, here's your new favorite cheese dip—extra garlicky, extra spicy. You may read this recipe and wonder, *Why whole walnut halves and not crushed walnuts?* Feel free to do with the walnuts what you will, but I love the way the crisped halves look when arranged over the glistening cheese, and the fact that everyone always joneses for them like the corner slices of a sheet cake.

Makes about 1¼ cups

---

1 teaspoon + 1 tablespoon olive oil, divided

¼ cup walnut halves

Small pinch of kosher salt

One 10-ounce log fresh goat cheese

2 garlic cloves, minced

1 teaspoon freshly ground black pepper

½ teaspoon red chile powder

1 Preheat the oven to 400°F.

2 In a small nonstick pan over medium-low heat, warm 1 teaspoon of the olive oil. Once the oil begins to shimmer, add the walnuts and cook, stirring, until the walnuts are lightly browned, 4 to 5 minutes. Turn off the heat and mix in the salt. Set aside.

3 In a bowl, mix together the goat cheese, garlic, and black pepper until homogeneous. Transfer to a 6- to 8-inch round or rectangular baking dish (no need to pat the cheese down) and bake for 20 to 22 minutes, until the cheese is bubbling and browned along the edges. Let the goat cheese cool for 5 minutes, then drizzle with the remaining 1 tablespoon olive oil and sprinkle the red chile powder and sautéed walnuts over the top. This dip is best eaten immediately—it doesn't reheat very well.

Clockwise from top left: Chile, Garlic, and Bay Leaf Olives (page 67); Spicy Chickpea Dip (page 58); Sun-Dried Tomato, Chile, and Garlic Dip (page 54); Spicy Olive Tapenade (page 51); Black Pepper and Chile Baked Goat Cheese; Lima Bean and Basil Dip (page 52)

Spicy Chickpea Dip

Makes 1½ cups

One 16-ounce can chickpeas, drained

¼ cup tahini

1 small Indian green chile or serrano chile, roughly chopped

1 garlic clove, crushed

3 tablespoons fresh lime juice (from about 1½ limes)

1½ tablespoons chopped fresh cilantro (stems and leaves)

1 teaspoon kosher salt, plus more if needed

2 tablespoons good olive oil, plus more for serving

½ teaspoon red chile powder, plus more for serving

My entire worldview changed when I went to Egypt at age nine. My sister and I were lucky enough to travel all over the globe with our parents, thanks to my mom's job working in software for the airline industry. On the vast majority of these trips, I was the disaffected kid in the back of the tour bus listening to the *Chicago* soundtrack, too distracted to pay attention to the sights. But Egypt was a game-changer: I got to climb inside the Pyramids of Giza, boat down the Nile River, and, last but not least, try HUMMUS for the first time. Not that packaged junk, but creamy, tangy, real-deal hummus, drizzled with really excellent olive oil and dusted with chile powder. My mom's take on a chickpea dip is inspired by one particularly glorious hummus we ate in Cairo, but with more heat, plus cilantro and plenty of lime juice—think hummus meets chutney. If there were ever a recipe to pull out your fanciest olive oil, this would be it. The good stuff makes an enormous difference.

1   Combine all the ingredients plus 2 tablespoons water in a food processor and pulse into a coarse paste. Taste and adjust the salt, if needed.

2   Transfer the dip to a serving dish and top with a drizzle of olive oil and a sprinkling of red chile powder. This dip keeps, refrigerated in an airtight container, for up to 1 week.

Tamarind, Fig, and Cumin Chutney

Makes 1½ cups

————

1 teaspoon ground cumin (freshly ground is best)

1 cup Maggi tamarind sauce (about half a 15-ounce bottle; see Tip) or ½ cup tamarind concentrate

2 heaping tablespoons fig jam

½ teaspoon red chile powder

This was one of those recipes that almost didn't make it into the book, because upgrading bottled tamarind sauce with fig jam and cumin is so second-nature to my mother that she didn't even think to suggest it. But like pretty much all of my mom's spur-of-the-moment culinary experiments, you're going to want to try this. Tamarind chutney is Indian cuisine's sweet-and-sour-sauce equivalent, and a perfect partner to most fried things. Adding a heaping spoon of fig jam and some freshly toasted cumin takes all of those amazing qualities of tamarind chutney and cranks them up—the sauce is tangier, sweeter, more lip-smacking. Drizzle it on a stir-fry, brush it on a pork loin, roll it up in a roti with some grains and pickled onions, bathe in it!

1 In a small saucepan over low heat, toast the cumin until it turns a shade darker, 3 to 4 minutes. Set aside in a small bowl and wipe out the pan.

2 In the same saucepan over medium-low heat, mix together the tamarind sauce and ¼ cup water (if using tamarind concentrate, up this to 6 tablespoons water) until fully integrated, then stir in the fig jam. When the sauce starts to bubble, stir in the red chile powder and toasted cumin and remove from the heat. Let cool for 15 to 20 minutes.

3 This chutney keeps, refrigerated in an airtight container, for up to 3 weeks.

tip: Look for Maggi tamarind sauce online or in any Indian grocery store.

Peanut Chutney

Makes ⅔ cup

——

½ cup roasted unsalted peanuts

2 small Indian green chiles or serrano chiles, halved and stems removed

One 1½-inch piece fresh ginger, cut into quarters

½ cup chopped fresh cilantro (stems and leaves)

1½ tablespoons fresh lime juice (from a little over half a lime)

½ teaspoon kosher salt, plus more if needed

Peanut chutney is a staple of South Indian cuisine—a chunky, bright, and satisfying accompaniment to dosa (a lentil-and-rice-based crepe) or idli (rice cakes). The problem is that many recipes for the chutney involve frying, lots of chopping, and using several different pans. Who has time to do all that for a single sauce?! Meet my mom's foolproof, streamlined, one-step peanut chutney. She's whittled the recipe down to her favorite components—the richness of the peanuts, offset by a few other bright, herby ingredients. It's nice and hearty because of the peanut base, and particularly fantastic for jazzing up a bowl of sticky rice or a plain ol' grilled chicken breast. Our personal favorite use is as a dipping sauce for Pesarattu (lentil pancakes, page 143), as the chutney gets all up in the pancakes' many crevices. The key is not to overblend—peanut chutney is best when you can still taste some coarse, peanutty bits.

1   Combine all the ingredients plus 3 tablespoons water in a blender and blend, occasionally using a spoon or small spatula to scrape down the sides, until the mixture resembles a chunky paste. If the mixture isn't blending properly, add a little more water a few drops at a time to get it going. Taste and adjust the salt, if needed. This chutney keeps, refrigerated in an airtight container, for up to 1 week.

Cilantro Chutney

Cilantro chutney is the king of chutneys. Why? Because it goes with any and all Indian food: samosas, dal, roti, any kind of chaat (the Indian genre of snacks) . . . you name it. During the photo shoot for this book, my mom churned out literal buckets of the stuff every single day because (1) it's delicious, (2) it's photogenic, and (3) we drizzle it on *everything*. I love this simple, OG recipe from my mom because it retains the pleasant grassiness from the cilantro and has a creeping, lingering heat (though you can nix the chiles if creeping heat is not your thing). There are also many ways to customize it—add mint for fresher notes, or nuts for richness. Use it as a salsa, a sauce for grilled chicken, or a topping for Roti Pizza (page 130).

Makes ½ cup (can be easily multiplied)

1 bunch fresh cilantro, preferably organic, stems and leaves roughly chopped (about 4 cups)

1 small Indian green chile or serrano chile, roughly chopped

2 tablespoons fresh lime juice (from about 1 lime), plus more if needed

¼ teaspoon granulated sugar

¾ teaspoon kosher salt, plus more if needed

tip: My mom prefers organic cilantro for this recipe, which she's convinced gives the chutney a more vibrant color and aroma.

1   In a blender, combine all the ingredients and blend until smooth. If the mixture is too thick to blend, add a few drops of water to get it going. Taste and adjust the salt and/or lime juice, if needed. This chutney keeps, refrigerated in an airtight container, for up to 2 days.

Garlicky Tomatoes

Makes 2 cups

4 medium Roma tomatoes, seeded, excess juice squeezed out, and cut into thin strips

2 garlic cloves, minced

1 teaspoon kosher salt

This is how you trick your sad, out-of-season tomatoes into thinking it's summer: Squeeze out their juice, cut them into strips, and give 'em a bath in garlic and salt. Suddenly, the tomatoes aren't limp produce—they're a flavorful condiment, adding the satisfying punch only a boatload of garlic can. Use this three-ingredient mix when you're throwing tomatoes on a salad, pizza, bruschetta, or sandwich. Nothing will ever replace the juiciness of a summer tomato, but this is a good back-pocket cheat for getting a little more sweetness and oomph out of less-than-ideal produce.

1   In a medium bowl, combine all the ingredients and toss to combine. Let marinate at room temperature for 1 hour before using. These tomatoes keep, refrigerated in an airtight container, for up to 2 days.

Green Chile and Cherry Tomato Pickle

Serves 4

——

2 tablespoons olive oil

¼ teaspoon fennel seeds

¼ teaspoon nigella seeds

¼ teaspoon cumin seeds

¼ teaspoon black mustard seeds

¼ teaspoon fenugreek seeds

¼ teaspoon asafetida (optional, but really great)

4 long Indian green chiles or serrano chiles, halved lengthwise (no need to remove the stems)

1 cup cherry tomatoes, halved

¾ teaspoon kosher salt

1 tablespoon fresh lime juice (from about half a lime)

Making *achar*, or pickle, is a long-standing Indian tradition. At the start of summer, my great-aunt will combine oil, vegetables, and a bunch of spices in a few jars, then set them out to marinate into a bright, spicy concoction during the warm months. This is my mom's shortcut pickle, which can function either as a condiment for rice and dal, or on its own as a tomato salad with a very big personality. It is the sweeter, cherry tomato version of an achar that's normally made with a sour tropical berry called karonda. Also, the specific combo of spices in here is called *panch phoran*, which literally translates to "five spices" and can be used in so many ways, from fish stew to dal. Other reasons to make this dish: (1) It comes together in less than five minutes, (2) it highlights the delightful flavor of good cherry tomatoes, and (3) it has the absolute BEST texture with all those crunchy seeds.

Unlike most achars, this one will not last in your fridge forever. Best to finish it off while it's fresh. And don't be afraid to eat the whole chiles—they get milder when they're cooked down.

1 In a large nonstick skillet over medium-high heat, warm the oil. Once the oil begins to shimmer, toss in the fennel seeds, nigella seeds, cumin seeds, black mustard seeds, and fenugreek seeds and cook until the spices look slightly browned and start to sputter (watch the cumin—that's the best indicator), about 1 minute max. Stir in the asafetida (if using) and then add the chiles. Cook for 2 minutes, until the chiles brown and crisp on the sides.

2 Turn off the heat, mix in the tomatoes, and immediately transfer to a serving bowl so that the tomatoes stop cooking. Gently mix in the salt and lime juice. Serve warm or at room temperature. This will keep, covered, in the fridge for a few days, but it's best polished off day-of.

Mango Launji

Makes 3 cups

———

2 tablespoons olive oil

¼ teaspoon fennel seeds

¼ teaspoon fenugreek seeds

¼ teaspoon cumin seeds

¼ teaspoon black mustard seeds

¼ teaspoon nigella seeds

1 teaspoon ground turmeric

¼ teaspoon asafetida (optional, but really great)

1 small Indian green chile or serrano chile, finely chopped

3 medium green (unripe) mangoes, peeled and diced into ¾-inch pieces (see Tip), pits discarded

1 teaspoon kosher salt

¼ cup packed dark brown sugar

There is a popular drink in India called aam panna—a refreshing combo of super-sour unripe mangoes, sugar, and spices meant to guard against heat stroke. Here all those ingredients instead make a chunky, stew-like, sweet-and-tangy chutney that probably won't help with heat stroke but will certainly liven up a pork chop or piece of toast. I first tried this phenomenal sauce at my great-aunt's house. I was slightly hungover and it was New Year's Day, and eating mango launji on puri (a type of fried bread) BROUGHT ME BACK TO LIFE. The recipe is dead simple once you've got the spices (and if you're missing one or two, that's totally fine). Also, if you can't track down green mangoes at the Indian store, those kinda shitty firm unripe mangoes on offer at most commercial grocers will get the job done. Want even more tartness? Decrease the brown sugar, and sub in cored and peeled Granny Smith apples for the mangoes.

1   In a medium pot or Dutch oven over medium-low heat, warm the oil, then add the fennel seeds, fenugreek seeds, cumin seeds, black mustard seeds, and nigella seeds. Cook for 1 to 2 minutes, until the fennel, fenugreek, and cumin seeds turn a darker shade of brown and start to sputter (watch the cumin—that's the best indicator). As soon as this happens, add the turmeric, asafetida (if using), and chile. Give everything a quick stir, then stir in the mangoes and salt. Add 1½ cups water and raise the heat to high to bring the mixture to a boil.

2   Once the mixture reaches a boil, lower the heat to medium, cover, and cook, stirring every 10 minutes to scrape up any bits that might be stuck to the bottom. Cook for 20 to 30 minutes, until the mango softens and becomes mushy, with a texture resembling chunky applesauce. Add the brown sugar and mix well. Remove from the heat.

3   Transfer to a medium container and refrigerate for at least 1 hour before eating. This sauce keeps, refrigerated in an airtight container, for up to 1 week.

tip: To peel the mangoes, slice the tops off and use a paring knife or potato peeler to peel the sides. To chop, place your knife about ¼ inch from the center and cut the cheeks off all four sides of the mango around the pit, then cut those cheeks into pieces.

Chile, Garlic, and Bay Leaf Olives

Serves 4

———

2 tablespoons olive oil

5 small garlic cloves, peeled

5 dried red chiles

4 bay leaves

1 cup green olives

¼ teaspoon red chile flakes

My mother's favorite section of Whole Foods is the olive bar, where you will find mounds of olives glistening with oil and herbs and garlic. The only problem with these mountains of olives is that, like everything at Whole Foods, they are overpriced. So here's a DIY, Indian-inspired way to make that bowl of party olives look and taste a lot more impressive, with dried chiles, bay leaves (which mellow out the saltiness of the olives), and browned garlic cloves that become gloriously sweet and mushy in the pan. If I have leftovers, I like to throw everything in a food processor, and then eat it with pasta, kind of like a lazy puttanesca sauce—just make sure you are using pitted olives if you do that.

1 In a medium nonstick skillet over medium-high heat, warm the oil. Once the oil begins to shimmer, reduce the heat to medium-low, add the garlic, and cook until the garlic is fragrant and starts to brown ever so slightly, 3 to 5 minutes. Add the red chiles and bay leaves and cook for another minute. Add the olives and cook until they are warmed through and slightly blistered, 2 to 3 minutes. Transfer the warmed olives, along with the chiles, bay leaves, and oil, to a serving dish and sprinkle with the red chile flakes. These olives keep, refrigerated in an airtight container, for up to 2 weeks, and can be easily rewarmed in a pan before serving.

VEGETABLE MAINS

Matar Paneer

Serves 4

¼ cup + 2 tablespoons ghee or olive oil, divided

4 green cardamom pods, or 1 teaspoon ground cardamom (freshly ground is best)

2 tablespoons coriander seeds

1 small yellow onion, roughly chopped

1 tablespoon roughly chopped fresh ginger

1 small Indian green chile or serrano chile, halved lengthwise and stem removed

7 medium Roma tomatoes, roughly chopped

1 teaspoon cumin seeds

2 bay leaves

½ teaspoon ground turmeric

¼ teaspoon asafetida (optional, but really great)

1½ teaspoons kosher salt, plus more if needed

8 ounces paneer, cut into ½-inch cubes (1 cup; see Tip)

1 cup fresh or frozen shelled sweet peas

½ cup chopped fresh cilantro (stems and leaves), for garnish

Serve with rice or roti

Matar paneer is the definition of a party dish. It's the sort of thing that you can serve to anyone—it looks really pretty and is always a crowd-pleaser (Cheese! Tomato sauce! Cumin-studded peas!). And it takes a *tiny* bit more effort than your standard Indian one-pan sabzi, which means you'll usually only pull it out when you want to impress a crowd. Typically, the paneer in matar paneer is deep-fried. But as my mom discovered, deep-frying at home sucks, and the dish ends up tasting a lot more balanced and not overly rich when the paneer is simply simmered in the pan with all the other ingredients.

tip: As soon as you cube the paneer, put it in warm water until you are ready to cook it—this will make sure it doesn't dry out. Just be sure to drain it before adding it to the pan.

1   In a large skillet over medium heat, warm ¼ cup of the ghee. Add the cardamom and coriander and cook, stirring, for about 1 minute, until they have lightly browned. Stir in the onion, ginger, and chile and cook until the onion is translucent, 5 to 6 minutes. Increase the heat to high, add the tomatoes, and cook, stirring, until the tomatoes are wilted, 5 to 6 minutes more. Remove from the heat and let cool to room temperature.

2   Transfer the cooled tomato mixture to a blender and blend into a chunky sauce—it should resemble baby food. If the mixture isn't blending well, add a few drops of water to get it going. Set the sauce aside.

3   In the same pan over medium-high heat, warm the remaining 2 tablespoons ghee. Add the cumin seeds and cook until they turn a medium shade of brown, about 1 minute max. Reduce the heat to low and add the bay leaves, turmeric, and asafetida (if using). Pour the sauce into the pan, add the salt, and mix well. Add the paneer, peas, and 1 cup water, cover, and cook for 10 minutes, or until the peas are warmed through and have nicely comingled with the paneer and sauce. Taste and adjust the salt, if needed. Garnish with the cilantro.

White Bean–Stuffed Poblanos

Serves 4

¼ cup + 1 tablespoon olive oil, divided

2 teaspoons cumin seeds

2 small yellow onions, finely diced

2 tablespoons ground coriander (freshly ground is best)

One 15-ounce can great northern beans, drained and rinsed

½ teaspoon kosher salt, plus more if needed

1 small Indian green chile or serrano chile, finely chopped

2 garlic cloves, minced

2 tablespoons fresh lime juice (from about 1 lime), plus lime wedges for serving

1 pound small poblano peppers of roughly the same size (2 to 3 ounces each), slit lengthwise

Find someone who looks at you the way my mom looks at poblano peppers roasting in the oven. She discovered poblanos a few years back, when she was perusing the grocery aisle for a spicy pepper that could work as a base for stuffed vegetables. She bought a few, threw them in the oven, and was thrilled with the result: smoky, earthy, and with a manageable but distinct heat. Part two of her big break-through: The first time she made them, she forgot to buy potatoes for the stuffing, so she subbed in white beans, mixing them with lots of garlic and cumin-coated onions. As it turned out, the white beans get even softer and creamier in the oven and absorb the flavors of the poblanos perfectly. File this dish under "recipes that look compli-cated but come together shockingly quickly." Also, the leftover white bean stuffing makes an excellent dip.

1   Preheat the oven to 350°F.

2   In a large skillet over medium-high heat, warm ¼ cup of the oil. Once the oil begins to shimmer, add the cumin seeds and cook until they turn a medium shade of brown, about 1 minute max. Add the onions and coriander and cook, stirring, until the onions are translu-cent, 5 to 7 minutes. Remove from the heat and let the mixture cool to room temperature.

3   While the onions cool, mash the white beans with a potato masher or fork in a medium-size bowl until they have the consistency of chunky mashed potatoes. Add the salt, chile, garlic, lime juice, and cooled onions and mix well. Taste and adjust the salt if needed.

4   Divide the filling evenly among the poblanos, using a small table-spoon to stuff the filling into each nook and cranny of the peppers.

5   Arrange the stuffed poblanos slit-side up on a baking sheet. Drizzle with the remaining 1 tablespoon oil. Bake for 45 minutes, or until the poblanos have shriveled and wrinkled at the area around the slits and turned dark green. Serve garnished with lime wedges.

Tofu Green Bean Breakfast Scramble

Serves 2

———

1 tablespoon olive oil

2 teaspoons cumin seeds

½ teaspoon ground turmeric

½ pound fresh green beans, ends trimmed, cut into 1-inch pieces, or frozen cut green beans (about 2 cups)

1 teaspoon kosher salt, plus more if needed

1 small Indian green chile or serrano chile, finely chopped

One 14-ounce package firm tofu, drained and crumbled into small pieces (think scrambled eggs for texture)

1 tablespoon fresh lime juice (from about half a lime), plus more if needed

2 teaspoons chaat masala, plus more if needed

Repeat after me: Don't scramble your eggs, scramble your tofu! This splendid breakfast dish is one of my all-time favorite ways to eat tofu. Oh, what's that? You hate tofu? *This* is the dish that has converted all of my tofu-skeptic friends. It's based on a classic Northern Indian breakfast my dad remembers from his childhood, originally involving crumbled paneer sautéed with spices and green beans and usually eaten atop toast. When my parents immigrated to America and my dad was craving this dish, tofu was my mom's workaround after not being able to find paneer anywhere. What she ended up discovering was how wonderfully light and bouncy the crumbled tofu gets, and how nicely that complements the crunch of the green beans. This dish is essentially a doppelgänger for scrambled eggs, thanks to the yellow color of the turmeric and the vaguely eggy, umami-like taste of the chaat masala. But tofu does a far superior job than eggs at really absorbing the flavor of the spices—plus, it's a lot harder to overcook tofu.

1 In a large skillet over medium heat, warm the oil. Once the oil begins to shimmer, add the cumin seeds and cook until they turn a medium shade of brown, about 1 minute max. Swirl the turmeric into the oil, then add the green beans, salt, and chile. Reduce the heat to low, cover, and cook for 5 to 7 minutes, until the green beans are just barely soft (they should still retain a bit of firmness).

2 Add the crumbled tofu and mix well, then increase the heat to medium and cook, uncovered, for 3 to 4 minutes, until the tofu has softened slightly and turned bright yellow from the turmeric. Remove the skillet from the heat and mix in the lime juice and chaat masala. Taste and adjust the lime juice, chaat masala, and salt before serving, if needed.

Bhindi (Charred, Spiced Okra)

Serves 2 to 4

2 tablespoons olive oil

1 teaspoon ajwain seeds

¼ teaspoon ground turmeric

Pinch of asafetida (optional, but really great)

1 small Indian green chile or serrano chile, finely chopped

One 12-ounce package frozen sliced okra (see Tip)

1 tablespoon ground coriander (freshly ground is best)

½ teaspoon fennel seeds

¼ teaspoon kosher salt, plus more if needed

½ teaspoon amchur (dry mango powder)

Serve with rice or roti

If you hate okra, I'm not sure we can be friends. In our extended family, this smoky, crispy okra is an iconic, clamored-after dish. When I was little, it was only made on special occasions, or when I was on my best behavior. It was a treat! I only recently found out that there are people out there who have only tried okra deep-fried (which is, of course, delicious, but must we deep-fry everything?), or who just really don't like okra because of its slimy texture. Herein lies the beauty of this recipe—you end up doing something close to dry-frying the okra, which dissolves any slimy texture and leaves you with slightly charred, flavor-packed little morsels. Also, AJWAIN: I'm pretty sure this oregano-like spice exists almost exclusively for okra. The pairing is truly supernatural.

> **tip:** Okra in ½- to 1-inch pieces works best. And fresh okra is fine, but we prefer frozen because it's faster! (My mom swears by the frozen packets at Indian grocers.)

1   In a large, shallow pan over medium heat, warm the oil. Once the oil begins to shimmer, add the ajwain seeds and cook until they turn golden brown, about 1 minute. Swirl in the turmeric and asafetida (if using), then add the chile. Increase the heat to high and toss in the okra, coriander, and fennel seeds. Stir gently using a flat spatula (you don't want the okra to become mush). Reduce the heat to medium, spread the okra in an even layer in the pan, and cook for about 10 minutes, flipping the okra pieces about halfway through so that both sides brown (a good way to flip the okra pieces without mashing them is to move the pan around in a circular motion). The okra may look gummy at first, and that's okay! Eventually, it will start to char.

2   Add the salt and cook for 5 minutes more—the okra should turn a dark shade of green and be lightly charred. Reduce the heat to low, add the amchur, and mix gently. Taste and adjust the salt if needed before serving.

Lotus Root and Jammy Tomatoes

———

3 tablespoons olive oil

1 teaspoon cumin seeds

½ teaspoon ground turmeric

5 whole cloves

Seeds from 3 green cardamom pods, crushed into a powder, or ¾ teaspoon ground cardamom (freshly ground is best)

1 medium yellow onion, finely diced

4 medium Roma tomatoes, finely diced

1 small Indian green chile or serrano chile, finely chopped

One 12-ounce package frozen sliced lotus root (¼-inch-thick discs are ideal; about 3 cups)

1 teaspoon kosher salt, plus more if needed

2 tablespoons chopped fresh cilantro (stems and leaves), for garnish

Serve with rice or roti

Have you tried lotus root? Any day now, I feel like it's going to become the new it-product at Trader Joe's. I can see the branding now: "A healthy veggie with a fun wheel shape and plenty of nooks and crannies for sauce!" But until the vegetable catches its big break, you can find it in Indian or East Asian grocery stores sold in presliced, frozen wheels. All you have to do is dump them in a pan and be patient. In this recipe, lotus root is paired with lots of tomatoes, which become super sweet and jam-like as they sweat in the pan, plus a potent, aromatic combo of cardamom and cloves. Remember that lotus root's natural texture is pretty firm even when it's cooked through—think water chestnuts or barely cooked potatoes, but in the best way possible. And if you don't feel like buying the lotus root (as many of my recipe testers told me), just make the jammy tomatoes and call it a day—they make an addictive spread or even a pasta sauce.

1   In a large nonstick skillet over medium-high heat, warm the oil. Once the oil begins to shimmer, add the cumin seeds and cook until they turn a medium shade of brown, about 1 minute max. Swirl in the turmeric and add the cloves, cardamom, and onion. Spread the onion in an even layer in the pan and cook until it just starts to caramelize, 6 to 8 minutes.

2   Increase the heat to high, add the tomatoes and chile, and cook, stirring continuously, until the tomatoes become soft and mushy, 4 to 6 minutes. Reduce the heat to medium-low and add the lotus root and salt, mixing them thoroughly into the tomato-onion mixture. Cover and cook for 30 to 35 minutes, until the lotus root is slightly soft and has a texture resembling a barely cooked potato (note that the lotus root will never become completely soft). Taste and adjust the salt if needed, then remove the skillet from the heat and let the dish sit for 10 minutes. Garnish with the cilantro before serving.

Spinach and Feta Cooked Like Saag Paneer

Serves 4

¼ cup + 2 tablespoons ghee or olive oil, divided

2 tablespoons coriander seeds

2 green cardamom pods, or ¼ teaspoon ground cardamom (freshly ground is best)

1 small yellow onion, diced into ½-inch pieces

1 tablespoon roughly chopped fresh ginger

1 garlic clove, minced

1 pound fresh baby spinach (10 to 12 cups)

½ tablespoon fresh lime juice (from about a quarter of a lime), plus more if needed

1 small Indian green chile or serrano chile, roughly chopped

1 teaspoon kosher salt

6 ounces feta cheese, cut into ½-inch cubes (a little over ½ cup)

1 teaspoon cumin seeds

¼ teaspoon asafetida (optional, but really great)

¼ teaspoon red chile powder

Serve with rice or roti

Here's a familiar Indian takeout staple—saag paneer—but with the ingenious substitution of large cubes of feta for paneer (a bit of inspiration from our 1998 family trip to Athens and near continuous consumption of Greek salads, which in Greece are just . . . salads). The first time I tasted it, it was like when I discovered you can do the 9 times table with your fingers in third grade, which is to say, I just about lost it. Not only is my mom's spinach gravy infinitely more complex than that of most versions of saag paneer (I have been known to steal sauce swipes out of the pan when my mom isn't looking), but I also love the way the feta gets all soft and pseudo-baked, soaking in all the spices and melting a little into the gravy. And then you hit the pan with the oiled-up cumin and red chile powder, which add a whole other level of richness. I would go as far as to say that I now want all future saag paneer I eat to be made with feta. And I bet you will, too.

1   In a large pan over medium heat, warm ¼ cup of the ghee (or oil). Once the ghee has melted (or the oil begins to shimmer), add the coriander and cardamom and cook, stirring, for about 2 minutes, until the seeds start to brown. Add the onion and cook until it is translucent, 5 to 6 minutes. Stir in the ginger and garlic and cook for 1 minute more. Add the spinach and cook until it is just wilted, 4 to 5 minutes.

2   Remove the pan from the heat and add the lime juice, green chile, and salt. Let cool for 5 minutes. Transfer to a blender and blend into a chunky paste. Return the spinach mixture to the same pan and set it over low heat. Stir in ½ cup water, then gently fold in the feta, being careful not to break up the cubes. Cook for 5 to 7 minutes more to soften the feta slightly and allow it to soak up some of the spinach sauce.

3   While the feta cooks, in a small pan or butter warmer over medium-high heat, warm the remaining 2 tablespoons ghee (or oil) for 1 minute. Add the cumin seeds. As soon as (emphasis on *as soon as*—you don't want your cumin to burn!) the cumin seeds start to sputter and brown, about 1 minute max, remove the pan from the heat. Immediately add the asafetida (if using) and red chile powder.

4   Pour all of the ghee (or oil) mixture into the spinach and feta once that is done cooking.

Whole Roasted Cauliflower with Green Pea Chutney

———

For the cauliflower

One 2- to 3-pound head cauliflower

¼ cup olive oil

Pinch of kosher salt

For the chutney

3 tablespoons olive oil

½ teaspoon fenugreek seeds

½ tablespoon whole black peppercorns

1 small Indian green chile or serrano chile, halved lengthwise and stem removed

2 garlic cloves, minced

1 small yellow onion, roughly chopped

1 cup frozen peas

¾ teaspoon kosher salt

½ cup chopped fresh cilantro (stems and leaves)

2 walnut halves

2 tablespoons fresh lime juice (from about 1 lime), plus lime wedges for serving

This recipe goes all the way back to 1980, when my mom and dad got married and bought their first cookbook, *The Pleasures of Vegetarian Cooking*, by the iconic and prolific Indian food writer Tarla Dalal (please stop what you are doing and Google this amazing lady, who published over one hundred books and is an absolute icon). Mom was looking for a vegetarian dish that could work as a dinner party show-stopper, and discovered this idea in Dalal's book. The chutney for this dish has evolved over the years as my mom has added little tweaks to make it really sing—but I'm obsessed with the current version, which is richer and heartier than your typical chutney thanks to the walnuts and peas, but still manages to taste light and bright. Eat the leftover chutney with anything and everything—grilled chicken, steamed rice, pasta, a piece of cardboard . . . you get the idea.

1   **BAKE THE CAULIFLOWER:** Preheat the oven to 400°F. Line a baking sheet with foil.

2   Place the cauliflower on the prepared baking sheet, evenly drizzle the ¼ cup oil over the top, and sprinkle with the salt. Bake for 40 to 50 minutes, until the cauliflower is golden brown and fork-tender.

3   **MEANWHILE, MAKE THE CHUTNEY:** In a large nonstick skillet over medium-high heat, warm the 3 tablespoons of olive oil. Once the oil begins to shimmer, add the fenugreek and peppercorns and toss in the oil for 1 to 2 minutes, until the fenugreek has lightly browned. Add the green chile, garlic, and onion and cook until the onion has become translucent, 3 to 4 minutes. Add the peas and cook until they are warmed through, 3 to 4 minutes more. Add ½ cup water and bring the mixture to a boil. Immediately remove the pan from the heat and stir in the salt and cilantro. Let cool for 5 minutes, then transfer to a blender. Add the walnuts and lime juice and blend into a smooth paste.

4   On a plate, make a pool of chutney and top with the whole cauliflower. To serve, slice the cauliflower into "steaks" of your preferred size and top with more chutney as desired. Garnish with lime wedges.

VEGETABLE SIDES

Chickpea Flour Green Beans

Serves 4

¼ cup chickpea flour

¼ cup olive oil

1 teaspoon ajwain seeds

1 teaspoon ground turmeric

¼ teaspoon asafetida (optional, but really great)

1 small yellow onion, finely diced

1 small Indian green chile or serrano chile, finely chopped

1 pound green beans, ends trimmed, cut into ½-inch pieces (see Tip)

1 teaspoon kosher salt

1 tablespoon fresh lime juice (from about half a lime), plus more if needed

I recently started seeing chickpea flour (also known as besan, or gram flour) *everywhere*. Now that apparently every child is gluten-intolerant, I see mommy bloggers hailing chickpea flour on their websites as this **breakthrough** discovery. I hate to break it to them, but Indians have been experimenting with this alternative flour for centuries. This recipe is my favorite use for chickpea flour—as a rich, crispy coating for vegetables. It's like tempura, but nuttier and without the greasy bits from the frying. This was also my late grandmother's absolute favorite dish, and geez, are these green beans good: crunchy on the outside, tender on the inside. It's all too easy to devour an entire pan of them in a single sitting. Make sure you scrape the roast-y bits off the bottom of the pan before serving. Those are the best part!

tip: Don't cut the green beans individually; it will take forever. Line up bunches of three or four beans of the same size and cut them together. Alternatively, just use frozen precut green beans—they work fine!

1   In a medium skillet over low heat, toast the chickpea flour, stirring continuously, until the flour is golden brown, 5 to 7 minutes. Transfer the flour to a plate and let it cool. Wipe out the skillet.

2   In the same skillet over medium heat, warm the oil. Once the oil begins to shimmer, add the ajwain seeds and cook until they start to pop, which should be in a matter of seconds. Swirl in the turmeric and add the asafetida (if using), onion, and chile. Cook until the onion is *just* translucent, 3 to 4 minutes. Stir in the green beans and salt, then the toasted chickpea flour. Add ¼ cup water and mix everything together so the flour evenly coats the beans. Spread the beans out into an even layer in the pan, cover, and cook for 5 to 7 minutes, until the beans are tender and bright green and there's a crispy layer of chickpea flour on the bottom of the pan. Once the beans are cooked, scrape up the crispy bits from the bottom of the pan and mix them into the beans. Remove from the heat and add the lime juice. Taste and add more lime juice, if needed, then give everything one last stir before serving.

Red Pepper, Potato, and Peanut Sabzi

My mom's cooking genius very often lies in the little things that turn otherwise ordinary weeknight staples into really distinctive dishes. That's the case in this recipe, where she takes the classic Indian marriage of snappy, sweet red peppers and crisped potatoes, and ups the ante with crushed peanuts and a spritz (or more!) of lime juice. The resulting colorful, crunchy, woken-up sabzi is an easy side that you can make in twenty minutes or less. You can also double it for an excellent vegetarian main course. Even better: Warm up some tortillas and scramble some eggs, and you've got yourself an Indo-Texan breakfast taco party.

Serves 4

2 tablespoons olive oil

1 teaspoon cumin seeds

1 teaspoon fennel seeds

1 small yellow onion, diced into ½-inch pieces

1 large russet potato, diced into ½-inch cubes

2 medium red bell peppers, diced into ¾-inch pieces

1 teaspoon kosher salt, plus more if needed

¼ cup roasted unsalted peanuts, crushed

1 tablespoon fresh lime juice (from about half a lime), plus more if needed

1 In a large skillet over medium-high heat, warm the oil. Once the oil begins to shimmer, add the cumin seeds and cook until they turn a medium shade of brown, about 1 minute max. Reduce the heat to medium and stir in the fennel seeds. Add the onion and cook until translucent, 4 to 6 minutes.

2 Stir in the potato, then spread the mixture into an even layer in the pan. Cover and cook for 7 to 10 minutes, until the potato is tender but not mushy (a little charring on the bottom is A-OK). Stir in the bell peppers and salt. Cover and cook for 5 to 7 minutes, until the peppers are slightly softened. Use a serving spoon or spatula to scrape up the delicious charred bits from the bottom of the pan and stir them into the dish.

3 Stir in the crushed peanuts and lime juice. Taste and adjust the lime juice and salt, if needed, before serving.

South Indian–ish Squash

Serves 4

———

2 tablespoons olive oil

1 teaspoon black mustard seeds

10 fresh curry leaves

1 teaspoon ground turmeric

¼ teaspoon asafetida (optional, but really great)

1 medium yellow onion, finely diced

½ small butternut squash, diced into ½-inch pieces (about 1½ cups)

1 medium zucchini, diced into ½-inch pieces

1 medium yellow squash, diced into ½-inch pieces

2 small Indian green chiles or serrano chiles, halved lengthwise (no need to stem them)

2 tablespoons ground coriander (freshly ground is best)

1 teaspoon kosher salt, plus more if needed

2 tablespoons fresh lime juice (from about 1 lime), plus more if needed

½ teaspoon red chile powder, plus more if needed

My mom's sweet-and-sour squash (page 115) is one of her oldest and most requested dishes. But just like you can't expect Beyoncé to sing "Single Ladies" at every single concert, my mom can't be held down to just one preparation of squash. That's where this many-textured and -colored recipe comes in, in which squash gets the Southern Indian flavor treatment, with earthy fried curry leaves, black mustard seeds, and coriander. The crunchy, astringent spices go great with the mellow sweetness of the squash (we like using three varieties for the color, but it's completely fine to stick to just one).

---

tip: Got leftover squash you don't know what to do with? Prick it a few times with a fork and roast it at 425°F for an hour, until fork-tender. Top with olive oil, salt, fresh lime juice, and red chile powder for yet another excellent squash-centric side.

---

1   In a large skillet over high heat, warm the oil. Once the oil begins to shimmer, add the black mustard seeds and as soon as they begin to pop and dance around in the oil, which should be within seconds, remove the pan from the heat. Add the curry leaves, making sure they get fully coated in the oil (there may be more popping and splattering, and that's okay!). The leaves should immediately crisp up in the residual heat. Return the pan to medium heat, add the turmeric and asafetida (if using), and stir to incorporate without breaking up the curry leaves. Add the onion and cook until it is translucent and starting to brown, 5 to 7 minutes. Add the butternut squash, zucchini, yellow squash, green chiles, and coriander and stir gently just to combine (be careful not to overmix, or you'll end up with mush). Spread the vegetables in an even layer in the pan, cover, and cook until the butternut squash is tender and soft, 8 to 10 minutes.

2   Add the salt, lime juice, and red chile powder and stir gently. Taste and adjust the lime juice, red chile powder, and salt, if needed, before serving.

Cheesy Chile Broccoli

This is the greatest hit among the classic make-the-kids-eat-vegetables-by-melting-cheese-on-top recipes my mom had in her parenting back pocket when my sister and I were growing up. The broccoli is dressed in that holy trinity of red chile flakes, garlic, and olive oil before it goes into the oven, which gives it a spicy, zingy flavor and crunchy crust *on top* of the salty, crispy, bubbly, melty coating of cheddar.

Serves 4

————

5 cups (½-inch pieces) broccoli florets and stems (from about 1 small head)

¾ teaspoon kosher salt

3 tablespoons olive oil

1 teaspoon red chile flakes

1 garlic clove, minced

¾ to 1 cup grated sharp cheddar cheese

1 Adjust an oven rack to the highest position and preheat the oven to 500°F.

2 In a large skillet over medium heat, combine the broccoli, salt, and ½ cup water. Cover and cook for 6 to 8 minutes, until the broccoli is just barely soft and the water has evaporated. Transfer the broccoli to a large bowl and set aside. Wipe out the skillet.

3 In the same skillet over medium heat, warm the oil. Once the oil begins to shimmer, stir in the red chile flakes and cook for 30 seconds. Add the garlic, return the cooked broccoli to the pan, and stir to combine.

4 Transfer the broccoli to a shallow 8- or 9-inch square baking pan and top evenly with the cheese, using more or less depending on how cheesy you like things. Switch the oven to broil and place the baking pan on the top oven rack. Broil for about 2 minutes, until the cheese is bubbling. Serve immediately.

Roasted Aloo Gobhi (Potatoes and Cauliflower)

Now, here's one you have probably heard of: aloo gobhi, the classic potato-and-cauliflower dish that's ubiquitous on Indian restaurant menus and in movies that feature an Indian family (I see you, *Bend It Like Beckham*). The problem is that most versions I've tried are overly mushy and way too heavy, usually from deep-frying. Enter my mom's simple but game-changing technique of *roasting* the cauliflower and potatoes before sautéing them, thereby allowing the vegetables to get that smoky, crunchy, charred exterior and also hold their shape in the pan without any excess oiliness. This is a great make-ahead party dish, as you can pre-roast the vegetables, and then whenever you're ready, throw them in the pan with your spices and onions to finish the dish in 15 minutes.

Serves 4

2 medium russet potatoes, cut into 2-inch-long sticks

1 medium head cauliflower, cut into small florets

3 tablespoons + 2 tablespoons olive oil, divided

1 teaspoon cumin seeds

½ teaspoon ground turmeric

1 small yellow onion, finely diced

Pinch of asafetida (optional, but really great)

Pinch of red chile powder

1 tablespoon julienned fresh ginger (see Tip, page 42)

1 tablespoon fresh lime juice (from about half a lime), plus more if needed

1 teaspoon kosher salt, plus more if needed

½ cup chopped fresh cilantro (stems and leaves), for garnish

1   Preheat the oven to 400°F. Line a baking sheet with foil.

2   Spread the potatoes and cauliflower over the prepared baking sheet and toss them with 3 tablespoons of the oil. Spread them in an even layer and roast for 30 minutes, or until the cauliflower and potatoes have browned and slightly crisped, tossing them once halfway through the cooking time. Set the vegetables aside to cool.

3   Meanwhile, in a large sauté pan over medium-high heat, warm the remaining 2 tablespoons oil. Once the oil begins to shimmer, add the cumin seeds and cook until they turn a medium shade of brown, about 1 minute max. Reduce the heat to medium and swirl in the turmeric. Add the onion and sauté, stirring, for 4 to 6 minutes, until the onion becomes translucent. Add the asafetida (if using), red chile powder, and ginger and cook for another minute.

4   Stir in the roasted potatoes and cauliflower, including any charred bits from the foil, and gently mix everything together (don't overmix, or the cauliflower will fall apart). Add the salt and cook for 5 to 6 minutes more, until the potatoes and cauliflower are tender (but not soggy!). Remove from the heat and add the lime juice. Taste and adjust the lime juice and salt, if needed. Garnish with the cilantro before serving.

Mushroom-Stuffed Mushrooms

Serves 4

———

16 small white button mushrooms (about 10 ounces; see Note), brushed clean

¼ cup olive oil, plus more for serving

1 small yellow onion, finely chopped

1 small Indian green chile or serrano chile, finely chopped

1 garlic clove, minced

1½ cups cooked white quinoa (from about ½ cup dry quinoa; see page 19)

¼ cup grated Parmesan cheese (1 ounce)

¼ cup chopped fresh cilantro

½ teaspoon kosher salt

½ teaspoon freshly ground black pepper

Here's an early '80s throwback you never thought you'd see in a cookbook called *Indian-ish*: dainty, appetizer-size stuffed mushrooms. Except unlike most of the disappointing versions you've tried from the frozen section of the grocery store, my mom's are so addictive that several mushroom haters who recipe-tested this dish admitted to me that they'd polished off a whole tray of them. The secret is stuffing the mushrooms with *more* mushrooms—specifically, chopped-up mushroom stems, which, along with quinoa, retain moisture and soak up the garlic juice and Parmesan cheese exceptionally well. If you've ever thought quinoa could only taste like bland rabbit food, this filling, which is basically like cheesy garlic bread in grain form, will change your mind. This recipe purposefully makes a little more filling than you need for stuffing the mushrooms, as it's perfect for snacking or taking for lunch the next day.

---

note: The mushroom caps should be small enough to eat in a single bite.

---

1 Preheat the oven to 350°F.

2 Remove the stems from the mushrooms. Set the caps aside, and finely chop the stems.

3 In a large pan over medium-high heat, warm the oil. Once the oil begins to shimmer, add the onion and chile and cook until the onion browns, 5 to 7 minutes. Add the chopped mushroom stems and cook until soft, 2 to 3 minutes. Stir in the garlic and cook for 1 minute.

4 Transfer the mixture to a large bowl and let cool for 5 minutes. Add the cooked quinoa, Parmesan, cilantro, salt, and black pepper and stir to combine.

5 Arrange the mushroom caps on a baking sheet and, using a teaspoon, fill them with the quinoa mixture—the filling should be spilling out of each cap.

6 Bake the stuffed mushrooms for 12 minutes, until slightly wilted and lightly browned on top. Let cool for about 5 minutes.

7 Drizzle each stuffed mushroom with a little olive oil before serving.

Tofu-Basil Endive Leaves

Serves 4 to 6

¼ cup pine nuts

3 tablespoons olive oil

1 small yellow onion, finely diced

7 ounces firm tofu (about half a 14-ounce package), drained and crumbled

¾ cup cooked basmati white rice (from about ¼ cup dry rice; see page 18), cooled to room temperature

1 teaspoon red chile flakes

1 teaspoon kosher salt

1 medium Roma tomato, seeded and finely diced

1 garlic clove, minced

10 large fresh basil leaves, finely chopped

16 endive leaves (see Tip)

For a long time, my mom was a regular at P.F. Chang's. Yes, you read that right: The lady who packs suitcases full of wine for trips (see page 189) can't get enough of that wok-fired cooking. She's been a fan ever since, at a work dinner, she discovered the lettuce wraps filled with spiced tofu. She loved that they were healthy but still flavorful, and that the chunks of tofu had this meaty craveability. Now that her office isn't near a P.F. Chang's, she doesn't really go anymore, but she has long held a soft spot for the joint. Inspired by those lettuce wraps, she came up with this "classy" (her word, not mine) version, which uses endive leaves and the Italian-leaning pairing of basil and garlic with the tofu as an homage to Mr. Chang (and tofu absorbs flavors QUITE well), plus rice for a bit of structure. This makes a very pretty party app, or you can nix the endive altogether and make the tofu and rice for a simple, filling lunch or snack.

tip: One whole endive will have more than enough leaves; radicchio also works.

1 In a nonstick medium skillet over medium-low heat, toast the pine nuts until lightly browned, 5 to 7 minutes. Transfer the pine nuts to a plate and set aside to cool. Wipe out the pan.

2 In the same skillet over medium-high heat, warm the oil. Once the oil begins to shimmer, add the onion, spread it in an even layer in the pan, and cook for 5 to 7 minutes, until translucent and lightly browned.

3 Add the tofu, followed by the rice and red chile flakes. Reduce the heat to medium-low and cook for about 5 minutes, until the rice and onion have nicely mixed and mingled. Stir in the salt and tomato. Remove from the heat and let the mixture cool for about 10 minutes. Stir in the garlic, basil leaves, and toasted pine nuts.

4 To serve, arrange the endive leaves cup-side up on a plate and divide the cooled tofu mixture among them.

Caramelized Ginger Mushrooms

Serves 4

————

3 tablespoons olive oil

1 teaspoon cumin seeds

1 medium yellow onion, finely diced

2 tablespoons julienned fresh ginger (see Tip, page 42)

1 small Indian green chile or serrano chile, halved lengthwise (no need to stem them)

1 pound white button mushrooms, cut into thin slices (about 5 cups)

1 teaspoon kosher salt

¼ teaspoon red chile powder

When my mom first gave me this recipe, I thought, *What's so great about mushrooms with ginger?* The answer, it turns out, is *everything*. This dish, based on a version my mom first tasted at a fancy hotel in Delhi, is so much greater than the sum of its parts—the mushrooms become sweet and caramelized, their natural funkiness tempering the intensity of the ginger. The depth of flavor in the dish feels improbable considering how little time and effort it takes to make. And aren't those the best kind of recipes? My mom told me to tell you that you can easily nix the onions in this recipe if you aren't a fan (though to that I would say . . . why did you buy an Indian cookbook if you hate onions?).

1   In a large nonstick skillet over medium-high heat, warm the oil. Once the oil begins to shimmer, add the cumin seeds and cook until they turn a medium shade of brown, about 1 minute max. Add the onion, spread it out into an even layer in the pan, and cook until lightly browned and translucent, 5 to 7 minutes. Add the ginger and green chile and cook for 2 minutes, until the chile is slightly wilted. Stir in the mushrooms and increase the heat to medium-high. The mushrooms will start to sweat. Cook until the mushrooms are browned and soft and the liquid they release has evaporated, 7 to 10 minutes. Add the salt and red chile powder.

Mustard Seed and Curry Leaf Carrot Salad

Serves 4

———

2 tablespoons olive oil

1 teaspoon black mustard seeds

8 fresh curry leaves

4 large carrots, grated

2 tablespoons fresh lime juice (from about 1 lime), plus more if needed

½ teaspoon kosher salt, plus more if needed

Tempered spices (aka chhonk, or tadka—see page 32) + lime + salt + grated raw vegetables = a quartet of freshness, texture, and balanced flavor—it will become your new go-to technique for salads. The key is choosing a vegetable that doesn't get super wilty and spices that will add texture but not overwhelm. Here's my favorite version, which uses carrots (their natural sweetness goes well with bitter, earthy spices), and the South Indian spice combo of mustard seeds and curry leaves. Try this with other vegetables—cucumbers, beets, and radishes would all work great—or test out another combination of spices, like cumin seeds, red chile powder, and dried red chiles. The mix-and-match possibilities are endless.

1   In a small pan over medium-low heat, warm the oil. Once the oil begins to shimmer, add the black mustard seeds and as soon as they begin to pop and dance around in the oil, which should be within seconds, remove the pan from the heat. Add the curry leaves, making sure they get fully coated in the oil (there may be more popping and splattering, and that's okay!). The leaves should immediately crisp up in the residual heat. Combine the carrots and the oil mixture in a bowl, add the lime juice and salt, and mix well. Taste and adjust the lime juice and salt, if needed.

Clockwise from top left: Basic Kachumber;
Beet and Avocado Kachumber; Mung Bean and
Potato Kachumber; Daikon Radish Kachumber;
and Avocado, Corn, and Tomato Kachumber

Kachumber (Salads!)

In India, salad is less of a thing. There are few colorful salad chains, and definitely no Internet memes of a girl laughing with a salad. Instead, there is kachumber. Kachumber means a lot of things to a lot of people, but the basic components are cucumbers, onions, and lime, served as a side to an Indian meal to counterbalance all those spicy, hearty stews and vegetables. Some people will just serve the raw vegetables on a plate and call it a day. My mom's kachumber is more like an Indian pico de gallo in its look and taste, and people go absolutely nuts for it. The secret? Raw garlic. It adds an indescribable depth and sweetness that only garlic can provide, with the lime juice obviating any unpleasant bite. Ever since I found this out, I throw raw garlic into all my salad dressings, and I encourage you to do the same.

Here's a recipe for my mom's basic kachumber, plus a few colorful variations she's come up with through the years that *loosely* fit under the same heading. Pro tip: The best part of kachumber is the salty, tangy, spicy juice that's left over at the bottom of the bowl. Do as the Krishnas do and pass the bowl around the table for slurping up that liquid gold!!!

Serves 4

5 medium Roma tomatoes, seeded and finely diced

1 Persian cucumber or ½ English cucumber, finely diced

1 small red onion, finely diced

1 small Indian green chile or serrano chile, finely chopped

⅓ cup chopped fresh cilantro (stems and leaves)

1 garlic clove, minced

1 tablespoon fresh lime juice (from about half a lime)

½ teaspoon kosher salt

BASIC KACHUMBER

1 In a medium bowl, combine the tomatoes, cucumber, onion, chile, cilantro, and garlic. Just before serving, add the lime juice and salt and mix well.

continued

BEET AND AVOCADO KACHUMBER

Serves 4

4 large or 6 or 7 small pre-cooked red beets (see Tip), diced into ½-inch pieces

2 tablespoons fresh lime juice (from about 1 lime)

1 small Indian green chile or serrano chile, finely chopped

1 garlic clove, minced

½ teaspoon kosher salt

2 just-ripe medium avocados, diced into ½-inch pieces

1   In a medium bowl, combine the beets, lime juice, chile, garlic, and salt. Just before serving, add the avocado and gently mix.

> **tip:** Precooked beets are typically available in vacuum-sealed packages at the grocery store—don't buy the canned pickled ones. If you can't find precooked beets, or just prefer to cook them yourself, preheat the oven to 400°F. Individually wrap each beet in foil (wrap them nice and tight, so no juice seeps out during cooking). Bake for 70 to 80 minutes, until you can easily pierce them with a fork, then let them cool completely.

MUNG BEAN AND POTATO KACHUMBER

Serves 4

1 medium russet potato, boiled (see page 20) and cooled

1 cup sprouted mung beans (see Tip)

1 small Indian green chile or serrano chile, finely chopped

1 small red onion, finely diced

¼ cup chopped fresh mint leaves

1 Persian cucumber or ½ English cucumber, finely diced

1 medium Roma tomato, seeded and finely diced

½ cup chopped fresh cilantro (stems and leaves)

½ teaspoon kosher salt

2 tablespoons fresh lime juice (from about 1 lime)

1 garlic clove, minced

1 just-ripe medium avocado, diced into ½-inch pieces

1   Peel the potatoes and use your hands to break them into ½-inch pieces. Put them in a large bowl, then add the sprouted mung beans, chile, onion, mint, cucumber, tomato, and cilantro and gently combine. Just before serving, add the salt, lime, and garlic, then carefully fold in the avocado.

> **tip:** It's best to buy mung beans at an Indian grocery store, where you'll find them pre-sprouted—all you have to do is toss them in the salad. If they're not already sprouted, follow the sprouting instructions on the back of the package.

1 large daikon radish (¾ pound), trimmed, peeled, and grated

1 small Indian green chile or serrano chile, finely chopped

2 tablespoons fresh lime juice (about 1 lime)

½ teaspoon kosher salt

2 tablespoons chopped fresh cilantro (stems and leaves)

DAIKON RADISH KACHUMBER

1 In a medium bowl, combine the grated radish, chile, lime juice, and salt. Fold in the cilantro and serve immediately.

1 ear corn, shucked, or about ¾ cup frozen corn kernels

4 medium Roma tomatoes, seeded and finely diced

1 just-ripe medium avocado, diced into ½-inch pieces

2 tablespoons fresh lime juice (from about 1 lime)

1 small Indian green chile or serrano chile, finely chopped

1 garlic clove, minced

½ teaspoon kosher salt

2 tablespoons chopped fresh cilantro (stems and leaves)

AVOCADO, CORN, AND TOMATO KACHUMBER

1 If using fresh corn, microwave the ear of corn for 4 minutes, until the kernels are soft and fully cooked. Set aside until cool enough to handle, then stand the cob in a medium bowl and use a sharp knife to cut off the kernels into the bowl. If using frozen corn, microwave until the kernels are thawed completely, and let cool to room temperature before adding to the bowl.

2 Add the tomatoes, avocado, lime juice, chile, garlic, and salt to the bowl with the corn and gently mix. Fold in the cilantro and serve immediately.

Lauki Sabzi (The Back-Pocket Gourd Recipe You Never Knew You Needed)

For my entire childhood, I was skeptical of lauki—a member of the gourd family that Indians often make into a quick, hearty sabzi on sick days and chilly nights. Most Indian kids hate it on principle: The color is uninteresting, it's not the kind of vegetable you can cover in cheese, and in Bollywood movies you only ever see elderly aunties and uncles eating it. But once again, my mom proved me wrong when, as an adult woman, I cooked her version—a deeply complex sabzi with buttery soft chunks of lauki and pleasantly sour notes from the tomatoes and lime. The ingredient list is short, and you can whip it up in twenty minutes and make a complete meal with rice or roti. If you don't feel like going all the way to the Indian grocery store for a gourd, zucchini works just fine!

Serves 4

———

3 tablespoons ghee or olive oil

1 teaspoon cumin seeds

1 teaspoon ground turmeric

¼ teaspoon asafetida (optional, but really great)

1 medium lauki (bottle gourd) or zucchini (½ pound), peeled (no need to seed it) and diced into ½-inch cubes

1 teaspoon kosher salt

2 medium Roma tomatoes, finely diced

1 tablespoon fresh lime juice (from about half a lime)

1 tablespoon chopped fresh cilantro (stems and leaves), for garnish

1   In a large skillet over medium-high heat, warm the ghee or olive oil. Once the ghee melts (or the oil begins to shimmer), add the cumin seeds and cook until they turn a medium shade of brown, about 1 minute max. Swirl the turmeric into the oil, then the asafetida (if using). Add the lauki and salt and toss to coat the lauki with the spices. Reduce the heat to medium-low, cover, and cook until the lauki can be easily pierced with a fork, 15 to 20 minutes. Add the tomatoes to the skillet, cover, and cook until the tomatoes are softened but not wilted, about 5 minutes. Stir in the lime juice and garnish with the cilantro before serving.

Dosa Potatoes with Lime and Ketchup

———

2 large russet potatoes, boiled (see page 20) and cooled

2 tablespoons olive oil

1 tablespoon black mustard seeds

10 fresh curry leaves

1 teaspoon ground turmeric

¼ teaspoon asafetida (optional, but really great)

1 small yellow onion, sliced into thin strips

1 teaspoon kosher salt

3 dried red chiles

¼ teaspoon red chile powder

Lime wedges, for serving

Ketchup, for serving

Masala dosas—large, thin, savory crepes typical of South Indian cuisine—are easily one of my top five foods, and it's all because of the filling: spicy, hangover-level comforting, semi-mashed potatoes. Dosas are often enormous and very difficult (for me, at least) to finish in one sitting. But I'll always polish off the potatoes. So my mom thought, *Why not make just the best part of the dosa?* Her version is sort of traditional (we're not South Indian), but with the worthy additions of lime and squiggles of ketchup—the former to cut through the richness of the potatoes, the latter because . . . potatoes and ketchup, of course!

1 Using your hands, break the potatoes into ½-inch pieces and set aside.

2 In a large skillet over medium-high heat, warm the oil. Once the oil begins to shimmer, add the black mustard seeds and as soon as they begin to pop and dance around in the oil, which should be within seconds, remove the pan from the heat. Add the curry leaves, making sure they get fully coated in oil (there may be more popping and splattering, and that's okay!). The leaves should immediately crisp up in the residual heat. Add the turmeric, asafetida (if using), and onion, return the pan to medium-high heat, and cook, stirring, until the onion starts to become translucent, 2 to 3 minutes.

3 Add the potato pieces, salt, red chiles, and chile powder, followed by ¼ cup water. Cover and cook until the potatoes are soft and slightly mushy but still retain some of their shape, 4 to 5 minutes.

4 Serve the potatoes with lots of lime wedges and ketchup to go on top.

Red Chile Potatoes

Serves 2

———

4 small new potatoes or baby red potatoes, boiled (see page 20) and cooled

¾ teaspoon red chile powder

¾ teaspoon chaat masala

1 tablespoon olive oil

1 tablespoon fresh lime juice (from about half a lime), plus more if needed

Kosher salt (optional)

In Indian culture, there is quite a lot of fasting. People do it for holidays, but they also do it on weekdays, months, or during specific time frames, sometimes for religious purposes and sometimes out of respect for spouses or elders and sometimes for reasons people can't even articulate to me. And "fasting" doesn't necessarily mean cutting out food: It can mean no sugar, no carbs, no alcohol, or having only boiled water between the hours of three and five p.m. My friend Khushbu told me she has a family friend who doesn't eat lemon on Fridays. I'm pretty sure Indians accidentally invented the crash diet?

My mom's fasting tradition is no salt on Tuesdays to honor her father's memory, and this recipe is her favorite fasting meal—a humble, nourishing bowl of broken potatoes seasoned simply with chile, oil, and lime juice. After my sister and I kept sneaking bites out of her Tuesday dinner, a salted, chaat masala–fied version of this dish eventually became part of our weeknight dinner rotation. This is not some fancy party showstopper, but it's wonderful in its simplicity, and too tasty not to share.

1   Using your hands, break the potatoes into ½-inch pieces and put them in a medium bowl. Add the chile powder, chaat masala, and oil and gently combine. Sprinkle the lime juice over the top. Taste, adjust the lime juice if needed, and season with salt, if desired—note that the chaat masala already has salt in it, so you may not need more.

Kaddu (Sweet-and-Sour Butternut Squash)

Serves 4

2 tablespoons olive oil

1 teaspoon fenugreek seeds

½ teaspoon ground turmeric

1 small yellow onion, finely diced

½ teaspoon red chile powder

¼ teaspoon asafetida (optional, but really great)

2 tablespoons minced fresh ginger

1 large butternut squash (about 2 pounds), peeled, seeded, and cut into ½-inch cubes

1 teaspoon kosher salt, plus more if needed

2 tablespoons fresh lime juice (from about 1 lime), plus more if needed

4 medium Roma tomatoes, diced into ½-inch pieces

2 tablespoons light brown sugar

2 tablespoons chopped fresh cilantro (stems and leaves), for garnish

You could say that this is the dish that launched the idea for this cookbook in the first place. Back when I was working at the food magazine *Lucky Peach*, I submitted this squash dish to my boss as a possible addition to our upcoming vegetable-focused cookbook. He and our recipe developer came up to me a few days later to tell me my mom was a gifted recipe writer, and that the kaddu—with its craveable sweet-and-sour flavor and sneaky complexity—was ingenious. For as long as I can remember, this squash has been a staple on our Thanksgiving table, which is usually a turkey-less, very quintessentially *Indian-ish* affair. It's my absolute favorite way to eat butternut squash, particularly when wrapped up in a puri (a type of fried bread), and served alongside the hearty potato-tomato stew Aloo Ka Rasa (page 116). But rotis or toast work beautifully as accompaniments, too. There are no bad ways to eat kaddu.

1   In a large, deep sauté pan over medium heat, warm the oil. Once the oil begins to shimmer, add the fenugreek seeds and cook until they start to sputter, which should be within seconds. Reduce the heat to medium-low and swirl in the turmeric. Add the onion and sauté until it just starts to soften, 3 to 4 minutes. Add the chile powder, asafetida (if using), and ginger and cook for 1 minute, then add the butternut squash and salt. Cover and cook until the squash is tender, 10 to 15 minutes.

2   Stir in the lime juice, tomatoes, and brown sugar. Reduce the heat to low, cover, and cook until the tomatoes are soft but still retain their shape, about 5 minutes more. Remove from the heat. Taste and adjust the lime juice and salt if needed. Garnish with the cilantro before serving.

Aloo Ka Rasa (Spicy Potato-Tomato Soup)

Serves 4

———

1 pound small new potatoes or baby red potatoes, boiled (see page 20) and cooled

1 tablespoon coriander seeds or ground coriander (freshly ground is best)

Seeds from 1 green cardamom pod, or ¼ teaspoon ground cardamom (freshly ground is best)

2 tablespoons ghee or olive oil

1 tablespoon cumin seeds

2 bay leaves

1 teaspoon ground turmeric

½ teaspoon asafetida (optional, but really great)

3 medium Roma tomatoes, diced into ½-inch pieces

1 tablespoon minced fresh ginger

1 small Indian green chile or serrano chile, finely chopped

1½ teaspoons kosher salt

¼ cup chopped fresh cilantro (stems and leaves), for garnish

I loved this rustic potato-tomato soup growing up because whenever my mom made it, that also meant we were having puri—flaky, deep-fried rounds of bread made in our house only for special occasions. I'd see the tangy soup bubbling away in the kitchen and immediately run outside to find my mom frying puri over our dinky outdoor stove (to prevent the oil stench from permeating the kitchen). As I got older, I soon realized that the soup—redolent of whole spices and as comforting as a pair of old sweatpants—was the best part all along, particularly when eaten alongside the sweet-and-sour squash dish Kaddu (page 115). That said, if there were ever a dish to inspire you to grab some frozen puris from the Indian grocery store (or tortillas from any store!), this would be it. With its thick, stewy broth and speckles of spices, this soup was practically tailor-made for sopping up with bread.

tip: Want to make the soup into a heartier meal? Add 1 cup cooked chickpeas, red beans, and/or pulled chicken or pork.

1 Peel the potatoes and use your hands to break them into ½-inch pieces. Set aside.

2 In a medium pot or small Dutch oven over low heat, toast the coriander and cardamom seeds until fragrant and lightly browned, 4 to 5 minutes. If using whole spices, transfer them to a spice grinder or mortar and pestle and grind into a powder. Set aside.

3 In the same pot over medium heat, warm the ghee (or oil). Once the ghee melts (or the oil begins to shimmer), add the cumin seeds and cook until they start to turn a medium shade of brown, about 1 minute max. Add the bay leaves, turmeric, and asafetida (if using), then immediately add the tomatoes, ginger, and green chile. Cook, uncovered, until the tomatoes are totally wilted, 7 to 10 minutes.

4 Add the potatoes, salt, and coriander and cardamom and stir until the potatoes are thoroughly incorporated with the tomatoes. Add 4 cups water, increase the heat to high, and cook uncovered for 7 to 8 minutes, until everything is fully integrated and the broth starts to thicken (while still remaining soupy). Turn off the heat, cover the pot, and let the soup rest for 10 minutes. Serve garnished with the cilantro.

Indian-ish Baked Potatoes

Serves 4

———

1 pound small new potatoes or baby red potatoes (about 12)

Kosher salt

¼ cup sour cream

4 teaspoons minced fresh ginger

½ small red onion, finely diced

2 small Indian green chiles or serrano chiles, finely chopped

2 teaspoons chaat masala

2 tablespoons chopped fresh cilantro (stems and leaves), for garnish

Of all the places my mom has traveled for work, her favorite will always be London—the cobblestone streets, the limitless sights, the walkability, and, most important, the pubs. She spent a lot of time in pubs on early '90s London business trips, and the only vegetarian dish (this was back when she was strictly veg) was very often a baked potato. This is where she discovered the ingenuity of filling a soft, steamy potato with all kinds of tasty toppings that absorb nicely into the starchy flesh. In this recipe, she subs out the big potato for smaller, thin-skinned ones (for a prettier presentation); and the bacon bits and chives and packaged cheese for spicier, brighter toppings: chiles, chaat masala, onions, and ginger. This dish takes almost no time to put together once the potatoes are baked, but looks very impressive as an appetizer or a small side. Also of note: The backdrop for this photo is the sari my mom was wearing when she first met my dad (right before their arranged marriage a week later). My heart melted a little when Mom told me that.

tip: Cut the ginger, onion, and chiles while the potatoes bake, so everything is ready for assembly.

1 Preheat the oven to 425°F.

2 Place the potatoes on a baking sheet and bake for 45 minutes, or until they can easily be pierced with a fork. Let the potatoes cool until they can be handled.

3 Without cutting all the way through to the bottom, slice each potato into four sections. Use your hands to push down and pull apart the four sections, like a blooming flower. Sprinkle a pinch of salt on top of each potato, followed by 1 tablespoon of the sour cream. Evenly divide the ginger, onion, green chiles, and chaat masala among the potatoes. Make it rain with chopped cilantro and serve.

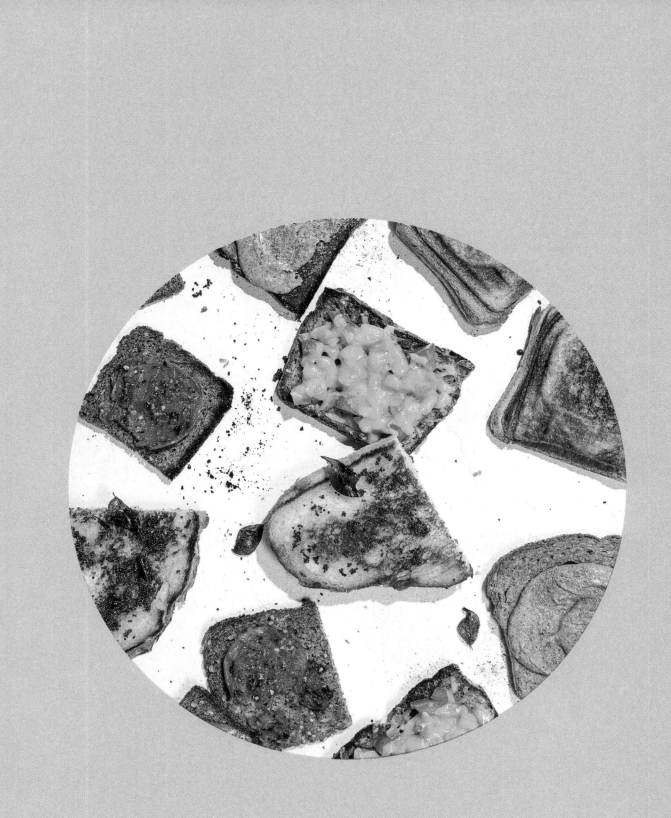

BREADS

Chaat Masala–Almond Butter Toast

Serves 1

———

1 slice bread (I like whole wheat)

2 tablespoons unsalted almond butter

¼ teaspoon chaat masala, plus more if needed

Yeah, yeah, almond butter toast. What else is new? Allow me to introduce you to the genius add-on of Indian cuisine's pungent, MSG-like spice blend, chaat masala, which turns an ordinary breakfast into an umami-filled salt-and-spice bomb that tastes like the most craveable nut mix in toast form. Just be doubly sure that you're using *unsalted* almond butter, as the chaat masala is already salted.

tip: Turn this into an appetizer—try the chaat masala–almond butter combo on rye crackers.

1   Toast the bread to the desired toastiness. Spread the almond butter over the bread, then evenly sprinkle the chaat masala over the top, adding more to taste.

Bombay Toast

Serves 1

½ cup leftover potato-based sabzi (Aloo Gobhi, page 96, is my personal favorite, but Red Chile Potatoes, page 114, and Dosa Potatoes, page 113, also work great)

2 slices multigrain bread

¼ cup grated cheddar cheese (1 ounce; optional)

Olive oil or butter, for cooking

Ketchup, for serving

Every Indian family has a go-to way of repackaging leftover sabzi into a portable meal; this is one of ours. This sandwich (FYI: Many Indians use the word "toast" to describe both toasts *and* pressed sandwiches) originated when my parents bought this particularly dope panini press that imprints a shell pattern onto the bread, and also seals down the edges so they get nice and crispy. My best memories of Bombay toasts are of making them the morning after Thanksgiving using leftover aloo gobhi, wrapping them in foil, taking them along to the Black Friday sales, and devouring them while perusing the racks. If you're like me and have a panini press collecting dust in the back of your cabinet, *this* is the recipe you should be bringing it out of retirement for. But don't worry if you don't have one—Bombay toast is foolproof no matter how you make it, and even more forgiving when dipped into ketchup (or Cilantro Chutney, page 62).

1 Mash the sabzi lightly with a fork to make it easy to spread.

2 Spread the sabzi evenly over one slice of bread, sprinkle with the cheese (if using), and top with the other slice. (Note that if you're making the sandwich in a pan, not on a panini press, it's worth including the cheddar cheese to help bind the sandwich together.)

3 **IF YOU HAVE A PANINI PRESS,** heat it on medium, swipe a little oil or butter over the plates, and press the sandwich until the bread turns golden brown with crispy edges.

4 **IF YOU DON'T HAVE A PANINI PRESS,** heat a skillet over medium heat, swipe the surface with a little oil or butter, and put the sandwich in the pan. Set a heavy plate on top to weigh it down and cook for a minute on each side.

5 Serve with a generous squiggle of ketchup.

Charred Tomatoes on Toast

Serves 1

———

¼ teaspoon olive oil

1 small Roma tomato (the more spherical, the better), halved

1 thick slice sturdy bread (such as multigrain or sourdough)

Kosher salt and freshly ground black pepper

This is a simple, clever breakfast technique that my mom discovered during her plentiful business trips to London as a software programmer. When she had morning flights out of Heathrow, she'd always sit down for a proper English breakfast: a platter of toast, baked beans, tomatoes, and mushrooms (no sausage; she's vegetarian). The tomatoes were always her favorite—she loved how charring the tomato made it mushy and spreadable, like a smoky, fruity condiment. Now I make these tomatoes at home at least three times a week. They're quick enough to make part of your daily breakfast routine, and elevated enough that you feel like you've made yourself a somewhat fancy English breakfast. For a spicy touch, add a sprinkle of chaat masala (in case you haven't learned already, chaat masala makes pretty much everything taste better).

1 In a small nonstick skillet over high heat, warm the oil. Once the oil begins to shimmer, add the tomato halves, cut-side down, and let cook, without stirring or moving them but occasionally pressing down on each half with a spoon or spatula, for 3 to 5 minutes. When the ends shrivel up and the bottoms begin to char, the tomatoes are done.

2 Meanwhile, toast the bread to the desired toastiness. Transfer the tomatoes to the toast, cut-side up, and smush them into the surface with a fork. Sprinkle with salt and pepper and enjoy.

Clockwise from top left: Charred Tomatoes on Toast, Chaat Masala–Almond Butter Toast (page 122), Bombay Toast (page 123), Tomato-Cheese Masala Toast (page 126), and Dahi Toast (page 127)

Tomato-Cheese Masala Toast

Makes 2 toasts (because that's usually how many I eat in one sitting)

———

2 slices bread, any kind (I like a very grainy bread, but this combo tastes great on truly anything)

1 medium Roma tomato, diced into ½-inch pieces

¼ cup grated sharp cheddar cheese (1 ounce)

½ teaspoon chaat masala, plus more if needed

Tomatoes, cheese, and toasted bread are three things that obviously taste good together. The wild card ingredient in this recipe is CHAAT MASALA, the funky, salty spice blend that brings this simple tomato-cheese toast to an entirely different level. It enhances the flavor of the already umami-filled ingredients and gives the dish a level of craveability that you just have to taste to believe. This dish is for my rough days, when there's nothing in my fridge except cheese and almost-overripe tomatoes and I want a five-minute dinner (or afternoon snack) that will still feel filling and satisfying. Also, just putting it out there: The best possible accompaniment to tomato-cheese masala toast is a glass of milk. Nothing else cuts through all that salt and keeps you refreshed between bites in quite the same way. Don't knock it till you've tried it!!!

1   Toast the bread to the desired toastiness. Evenly top each piece of toast with the tomatoes, followed by the cheese.

2   Place the tomato-cheese toasts in a toaster oven (or under the broiler on high) and toast until the cheese has fully melted on top of the tomatoes. (Alternatively, microwave the toasts on high in 30-second intervals, until the cheese has fully melted on top of the tomatoes.)

3   Sprinkle the toasts with the chaat masala, adding more to taste.

Dahi Toast (Spiced Yogurt Sandwich)

Out of all my mom's greatest breakfast hits, dahi toast is easily the most the beloved in our family. This sandwich—a loose interpretation of a recipe from one of my dad's friends—is totally unexpected (who would ever think to put yogurt between bread?!) and impossible not to like. Imagine a tangier, spicier grilled cheese sandwich. You get that satisfying oily bread crunch, but with onions, chiles, and (my favorite part) a crispy topping of black mustard seeds and curry leaves added into the mix. The glue that holds this recipe together is the tang of the sourdough bread—it's the perfect foil to the rich, ricotta-like filling. We are a house divided when it comes to accompaniments for dahi toast—my mom and sister like cilantro chutney, while I prefer ketchup. My dad uses both: He swirls the chutney and ketchup together to create a kinda ugly-colored but admittedly delicious super-sauce.

Makes 6 sandwiches

———

¼ cup olive oil, plus more for cooking the toasts

1½ teaspoons black mustard seeds

3 sprigs fresh curry leaves, stripped (24 to 30 leaves)

1 cup low-fat plain Greek yogurt

½ medium red onion, finely diced

½ cup finely chopped fresh cilantro (stems and leaves)

2 small Indian green chiles or serrano chiles, finely chopped

1 teaspoon kosher salt

½ teaspoon freshly ground black pepper

Pinch of red chile powder

12 large slices white sourdough bread

Ketchup, for serving (optional)

Cilantro Chutney (page 62), for serving (optional)

1 In a butter warmer or small pan over low heat, warm the oil. Once the oil is warm but not super hot, add the black mustard seeds and as soon as they begin to pop and dance around in the oil, which should be within seconds, remove the pan from the heat. Add the curry leaves, making sure they get fully coated in the oil (there may be more popping and splattering, and that's okay!). The leaves should immediately crisp up in the residual heat. Set aside.

2 In a small bowl, mix together the yogurt, onion, cilantro, green chiles, salt, black pepper, and red chile powder. Spread the yogurt mixture over 6 slices of the bread and top with the remaining slices to make 6 sandwiches.

3 In a large pan over medium heat, warm 1 teaspoon oil. Once the oil begins to shimmer, reduce the heat to low and add as many sandwiches as will fit in the pan. Cook until the undersides are crisp and lightly browned, 3 to 4 minutes, then flip them, add another teaspoon of oil to the pan, and cook until the other side is crisp and slightly browned, 3 to 4 minutes more. Transfer the sandwiches to a platter and repeat to cook the remaining sandwiches.

4 Divide the spiced oil mixture evenly over the top of the sandwiches. Cut each sandwich in half and serve immediately with a side of ketchup and/or chutney, if desired.

Roti Pizza

Back when my sister and I were younger, brattier, and far less appreciative of my mother's amazing cooking, we would beg my mom to let us order pizza for dinner. Instead of giving in to our demands, she came up with this compromise: our favorite pizza toppings, but on roti. As it turns out, roti makes an excellent pizza crust—it chars and crisps up nicely, and it doesn't get soggy under the weight of the toppings. Roti pizza is now the most-made dish in our house, and we've gotten really creative with topping variations. We've graduated from mozzarella and tomato and moved toward newer discoveries, like potatoes, rosemary, and Parmesan (an innovative Spanish-slash-Italian pizza), or chutney, cheddar, and onion (salty, spicy, and very addictive). Feel free to get as creative as you want! Try making it with sweet ingredients, like cinnamon-sprinkled apples or Nutella and strawberries. Roti pizza parties are for all.

Serves 2

———

Four 7-inch rotis or whole wheat tortillas (use 8 rotis if you are making both variations)

Olive oil, for drizzling

For the chutney-cheddar topping

1 small red onion, halved and thinly sliced

1 cup shredded sharp cheddar cheese (4 ounces)

2 tablespoons Cilantro Chutney (page 62)

For the potato-rosemary topping

1 medium russet potato, sliced into paper-thin rounds (a mandoline works best for this)

1 cup grated Parmesan cheese (4 ounces)

2 tablespoons roughly chopped fresh rosemary

1 Preheat the oven to 400°F.

2 Score each roti a few times with a knife or fork. Place them on a perforated pizza pan or a broiler pan. Drizzle olive oil on each roti (enough to coat the roti but not soak it) and smooth the oil over the surface with your fingers. Bake for 4 to 6 minutes, until lightly golden brown. Remove from the oven but keep the oven on. Once more, drizzle each baked roti with a little olive oil (again, enough to coat but not soak the roti) and smooth it over the surface with your fingers.

3 **TO MAKE CHUTNEY-CHEDDAR PIZZAS:** Evenly distribute the onion among the rotis, followed by the cheddar. Bake for 5 to 7 minutes, until the cheddar is melted and bubbling and the edges are crisp. Remove the pizzas from the oven, let cool for 2 to 3 minutes, then drizzle them with the chutney.

4 **TO MAKE POTATO-ROSEMARY PIZZAS:** Layer the potato slices over the rotis, and top with another small drizzle of olive oil. Bake for 5 minutes, until the potatoes are soft and fully cooked. Distribute the cheese evenly over the rotis and bake for 5 minutes more, until the cheese has crisped up at the edges. Remove the pizzas from the oven, sprinkle with the rosemary, and drizzle a little more olive oil on top.

5 Cut the roti pizzas into quarters.

Roti Noodle Stir-Fry

Serves 4

————

Four 7-inch rotis or whole wheat tortillas (look for tortillas on the thinner side)

3 tablespoons olive oil

12 fresh curry leaves

2 small Indian green chiles or serrano chiles, finely chopped

½ medium red onion, cut into 2-inch strips

1 medium red bell pepper, cut into 2-inch matchsticks

1 medium green bell pepper, cut into 2-inch matchsticks

½ small green cabbage, shredded

1 large carrot, grated

½ teaspoon kosher salt, plus more if needed

2 tablespoons fresh lime juice (from about 1 lime), plus more if needed

2 tablespoons chopped fresh cilantro (stems and leaves), for garnish

¼ cup roasted unsalted peanuts, crushed, for garnish

This recipe is the result of a trip my mom took to Sri Lanka with her friend Sunitha while I was in the midst of writing this book. When she came back, she breathlessly insisted that we needed to publish a version of this colorful street food stir-fry she'd tried called kottu roti, made by tossing strips of roti, spices, and vegetables in a hot wok. My mom's version has the addictiveness of a late-night plate of nachos but still feels very wholesome. I'm calling this inauthentic take "Roti Noodle Stir-Fry," because I love how the roti strips turn soft, chewy, and pliable (like noodles!) in the pan. And, because it's my mom, this adaptation has triple the vegetables (totally worth the chopping effort, I promise) you'd probably get in the street food version, making it a wonderful healthy weeknight meal.

1   Stack the rotis on top of one another and cut them in half. Cut the roti halves into ¼-inch-wide strips.

2   In a large nonstick skillet or wok over medium-high heat, warm the olive oil. Once the oil begins to shimmer, add the curry leaves and green chiles, tossing for a few seconds to coat them in the oil. Increase the heat to high and add the onion. Cook until the onion just begins to wilt, about 30 seconds, then add the red and green bell peppers and cook until *they* just begin to wilt, 30 seconds more. Add the cabbage and carrot, then stir in the roti pieces and cook for 1 to 2 minutes, until the roti is soft and noodle-like. Add the salt and turn the heat off. Stir in the lime juice. Taste and adjust the lime juice and salt if needed, then garnish with the cilantro and peanuts.

Roti Roli Poli

————

4 rotis or whole wheat tortillas

Salted butter, for spreading

½ cup sabzi (any of the ones in this book will work—we love Aloo Gobhi, page 96, Dosa Potatoes, page 113, Kaddu, page 115, or Bhindi, page 76)

4 tablespoons Cilantro Chutney (page 62; optional)

My family never purchases food at airports or train stations—it's a holdover from my mom's paranoia about what she perceived to be the loose hygiene standards at Indian train station kiosks. So instead, when I was growing up, whenever we would travel my mom would take whatever leftover *sabzi* we had in the fridge, roll it up into rotis, and wrap them in foil like taquitos. While everyone else on the plane suffered through their disappointing, overpriced airport BLTs, we'd devour our delicious teensy burritos, which my mom dubbed "Roti Roli Polis" because they are shaped like the roly-poly bugs that are ubiquitous in Texas. These are the ideal travel food: They are small and portable, they don't leak, and they are so filling! One day, I'll buy a billboard outside of every airport, and they will all say: "DON'T GET DUPED BY AN AIRPORT KIOSK SANDWICH AGAIN: EAT A ROTI ROLI POLI."

1   Warm a small nonstick pan over medium heat. Once the pan is thoroughly hot (2 to 3 minutes), add a roti and cook for 1 minute on each side, until the roti has some dark brown spots and becomes soft and puffy. Transfer to a plate and repeat with the remaining rotis.

2   Spread a thin layer of butter over the surface of one side of each roti, then spread 2 tablespoons of the sabzi right down the middle and top with 1 tablespoon of the chutney (if using). Roll each roti snugly around the filling. If transporting the rotis, wrap them (tightly!) in foil. They will keep at room temperature for up to a day.

Pav Bhaji on Potato Rolls

Serves 4

———

For the bhaji (vegetables)

¾ cup frozen or fresh cauliflower florets

½ cup frozen peas

2 medium russet potatoes, boiled (see page 20) and cooled

1 tablespoon olive oil

¾ teaspoon ground turmeric

1 tablespoon ground coriander (freshly ground is best)

¼ teaspoon red chile powder

2 large Roma tomatoes, diced into ½-inch pieces

1 (or 2, if you like it spicy!) small Indian green chile or serrano chile, finely chopped

1½ teaspoons kosher salt, plus more if needed

¼ cup chopped fresh cilantro (stems and leaves)

For the pav

8 hamburger buns (preferably Martin's potato rolls or other potato rolls)

Salted butter, for bun-buttering

½ medium red onion, finely diced

Lime juice, plus wedges for serving

If my cousin Isha could eat one food for the rest of her life, it would be pav bhaji—a sloppy joe–like party food of buttered buns slathered in spicy vegetable gravy and topped with lime and onions. This is probably because her mom, my aunt Sonia, makes the greatest pav bhaji . . . and the recipe just so happens to be shockingly simple (Can you boil vegetables? You can make this recipe!). The proportion of veggies to spices is spot on, the gravy is sharp and aromatic but not overly greasy like a lot of Indian restaurant versions, and it's made with good ol' fashioned potato rolls, which are the squishiest king of buns. The best part, though, is that pav bhaji is the most forgiving of all the recipes in this cookbook. Even if you mess up the gravy or accidentally undercook the potatoes, you are ultimately topping it all off with lime and onions and serving it in buttered potato rolls, and that's always going to taste really, really good.

1   MAKE THE BHAJI (VEGETABLES): In a small pot, combine the cauliflower, peas, and 3 cups water and bring to a boil over high heat. Reduce the heat to medium-high, cover, and cook until the cauliflower is soft and fork-tender, 7 to 10 minutes. Thoroughly drain, then return the vegetables to the pot and use a potato masher or fork to lightly mash them (they should still be chunky, just more incorporated). Set aside.

2   Peel the potatoes, put them in a bowl, and use the potato masher or a fork to mash them (don't worry if there are still a few small lumps). Set aside.

3   In a medium pan over medium-high heat, warm the oil. Once the oil begins to shimmer, swirl in the turmeric. Add the coriander, red chile powder, and tomatoes and cook until the tomatoes have started to soften, 3 to 4 minutes. Reduce the heat to low, add 2 tablespoons water and the green chile, and simmer for about 4 minutes, using a spoon or spatula to mash the tomatoes into a chunky sauce as they cook.

continued

Pav Bhaji on Potato Rolls, continued

4   Add the mashed potatoes, the cauliflower-pea mixture, the salt, and ¼ cup water. Increase the heat to medium-low and cook until the mixture starts to resemble a thick stew, 5 to 7 minutes. Add more water, 1 tablespoon at a time, if it's looking too dry. Taste and adjust the salt if needed. Stir in the cilantro, turn off the heat, and transfer the bhaji to a bowl. Wipe out the pan.

5   **MAKE THE PAV:** Split each bun in half and butter each side. Warm the pan you used for the bhaji over high heat and toast the buns in the pan, buttered-side down, until golden brown, about 1 minute.

6   **ASSEMBLE THE PAV BHAJI:** Evenly portion the bhaji on each bun half (like an open-faced sandwich) and top each with a tablespoon of diced onion plus a generous squeeze of lime juice. Serve with the remaining onion and lime wedges alongside.

Eggless Pancakes

Makes 2 medium or 4 small pancakes

――――

½ cup Bisquick

2 teaspoons ground flaxseed

1 teaspoon wheat germ

½ cup 2% milk, plus more if needed

2 tablespoons dark chocolate chips (optional)

Salted butter, at room temperature, for serving

During weekends growing up, my sister and I—ever the American kids just wanting to eat what our white friends did—always demanded pancakes. So my mom reluctantly purchased a box of Bisquick, scanned the pancake recipe on the back of the package, and made some inspired tweaks: She nixed the eggs (many Indian sweets avoid egg, as a general thing; see also the cake on page 205), and added wheat germ and flaxseed to up the nutrition factor in a sneaky, undetectable way. The resulting pancakes were so improbably, alchemically fluffy and wholesome that they became legendary among our cousins, friends, and neighbors—*to this day*, people tell me those pancakes are still hands-down the best they've ever had—and it doesn't make any sense because they have no eggs and are made with a packaged mix. Whenever all our cousins come home for the holidays, there is always a pancake breakfast at our house. My mom makes these massive pancakes and serves them to the cousins in order from youngest to oldest, and because I'm the second oldest, I'm inevitably full by the time she gets to me because I've stolen bites of everyone else's breakfast.

tip: Nothing but Bisquick will do for this recipe—we've tried using whole ingredients and other mixes, and it's just not the same!

1 Warm a large nonstick pan over medium heat. While the pan heats up, combine the Bisquick, flaxseed, and wheat germ in a measuring cup with a spout (for easy pouring). Add the milk—the consistency should be thick but pourable. Fold in the chocolate chips (if using).

2 Pour the batter into the preheated pan in a large, round circle (or two smaller circles). Once lots of bubbles form on the top and along the edges of the pancake, anywhere from 2 to 5 minutes, use a wide spatula to flip it over and cook until the underside is golden brown, 1 to 3 minutes more. Flip one more time to ensure that both sides are golden brown. Don't press down on the pancake with a spatula, as that will release air and make it less fluffy!

3 Just before the pancake is finished cooking, spread some butter across the top while it's still in the pan, then transfer to a plate. Repeat with remaining batter. If the batter gets too thick as it sits, stir in more milk, 1 tablespoon at a time, until it's pourable again.

4 Serve warm, with more butter alongside.

Herby Avocado Sandwich

Once upon on a time, my mom was quickly throwing together lunch before running off to catch a flight. In a pho-inspired impulse, she grabbed some leftover herbs that were about to go bad from the fridge and tossed them into her everyday sandwich of sliced avocado and tomato. The herbs brightened and lightened the sandwich in the most wonderful way, giving it a slightly fancier, vaguely cheffy edge. Now we can't eat our avo sandwiches any other way.

Serves 1

2 slices sourdough or whole wheat bread

Olive oil

½ just-ripe medium avocado, cut into long slices

Kosher salt

1 small Roma tomato, sliced into thin rounds

Freshly ground black pepper

Leaves from 2 sprigs fresh cilantro

Leaves from 2 sprigs fresh mint

1 Toast the bread to the desired toastiness.

2 Drizzle both slices of bread lightly with olive oil. Place the avocado on one of the slices and mash it with a fork so that it sticks to the bread. Sprinkle a little bit of salt on top of the avocado, then layer on the slices of tomato, followed by another sprinkle of salt and a few cranks of pepper. Arrange the cilantro and the mint on top and finish with the other slice of bread, oiled-side down, pressing gently.

Pesarattu (Lentil Pancakes)

Makes 7 or 8 pancakes, to serve 2 or 3

―――

1 cup split green mung beans

1 tablespoon minced fresh ginger

1 teaspoon kosher salt, plus more if needed

1 small Indian green chile or serrano chile, finely chopped

¼ cup vegetable oil

15 fresh curry leaves, torn into 2 or 3 pieces each

½ medium red onion, finely diced

Here's something you can do with lentils other than turning them into a soup: Make them into a healthy, savory, ginger-and-chile-infused pancake. My mom first ate this dish at her friend Madhu's house, and she was surprised by (1) how easy the pancakes were to make (just be sure to plan ahead for the overnight soaking of the mung beans) and (2) how crazy-flavorful they were, despite the fact that they were made entirely out of lentils. These pancakes pack enough of a punch that you can eat them by themselves (and you can eat *a lot* in one sitting because . . . it's just lentils!), but might my mom and I suggest a side of PEANUT CHUTNEY (page 61), the chunky, herby, good-on-everything sauce?

1   In a medium bowl, soak the mung beans in 2 cups water overnight.

2   Drain and rinse the mung beans, then transfer them to a blender and add the ginger, salt, green chile, and 1 cup water. Blend until the mixture forms a pasty batter, with tiny flecks of mung bean visible. Transfer the batter to a bowl.

3   In a large nonstick skillet over medium-high heat, warm 2 teaspoons of the oil. Once the oil begins to shimmer, pour ⅓ cup of the batter into the skillet, spreading it out with the back of a spoon to make a thin, 7- to 8-inch pancake. Sprinkle a few curry leaf pieces and 2 teaspoons of the onion (or more, if you really like onions) over the top of the pancake. Reduce the heat to medium and cook the pancake until the edges are slightly crisp, 3 to 4 minutes. Flip the pancake and cook for 3 to 4 minutes more, until the onion on the underside is brown. Flip the pancake one more time and cook for another minute if you want the edges to be extra crispy. Sprinkle the finished pancake with a little salt, then transfer to a plate. Repeat with the remaining batter, curry leaves, and onion, adding 2 teaspoons oil to the pan between each batch.

Aloo (Potato) Parathas

――――

For the dough

1 cup whole wheat flour, plus more for dusting

½ cup room-temperature water

¼ teaspoon vegetable oil

¼ teaspoon kosher salt

For the filling

2 medium russet potatoes, boiled (page 20), cooled, and peeled

¼ teaspoon red chile powder

¾ teaspoon fennel seeds, crushed into a powder (this is easiest in a mortar and pestle)

2 tablespoons chopped fresh cilantro (stems and leaves)

½ teaspoon kosher salt

¼ cup vegetable oil, for basting the paratha (set aside in a small bowl for easy access)

When I go back home to Dallas, my priorities are usually something like the following: Get eyebrows threaded, go to the Galleria mall with mom, and eat aloo parathas at my aunt Rachna's house. I typically text Rachna, who is one of my mom's sisters-in-law, the minute I land at DFW airport, and we set a date for me to come over and eat aloo parathas while we gossip about her son Ruchir's love life. Aloo parathas are a simple dish—just bread filled with potatoes and spices. But the beauty of Rachna's aloo parathas is the ratio. You know how people always complain that crab cakes have too much breading and not enough crab? This is also a common complaint about aloo parathas: too much dough, too little potato. Rachna's version, however, is about 80 percent potato, 20 percent dough—the ideal proportions for ensuring a soft, satiny paratha. There are a lot of steps, but don't be intimidated! If you can operate a rolling pin, you can make paratha. And when serving these, our family doesn't abide by any kind of formalities—as soon as one is ready, someone claims it so it can be eaten while piping hot, with Cilantro Chutney (page 62) or whatever condiment (achar, raita, etc.) happens to be around that day.

tip: Want to give your aloo paratha a little twist? Add ¼ cup grated cheddar cheese to the potatoes in step 2.

1   MAKE THE DOUGH: In a medium bowl, mix all the dough ingredients together and knead the dough with your hands until it is smooth and well incorporated. The dough should be soft, slightly sticky, and not too wet. Wrap the dough in plastic wrap and refrigerate for 20 minutes.

2   WHILE THE DOUGH IS RESTING, MAKE THE FILLING: In another medium bowl, using your hands or a potato masher, mash the potatoes, then use a wooden spoon or spatula to fold in the red chile powder, fennel, cilantro, and salt. Aim for the consistency of smooth mashed potatoes. (If the potatoes aren't smooth enough, the dough will be hard to roll.) Use a fork to get rid of any lumps.

3   Divide the dough and mashed potatoes into 4 equal portions (as in, 4 portions of dough and 4 portions of potatoes) and roll each portion into a ball.

continued

Aloo Parathas, continued

4   Generously sprinkle a clean work surface with flour. Lightly coat each dough ball with flour, then use a rolling pin to roll out each ball into a 6-inch circle, rotating the dough as you roll to maintain the circular shape, and adding more flour to your work surface as needed to prevent sticking.

5   Working one at a time, place a potato ball in the center of a dough circle, then pull the edges of the dough over the top of the ball, like you would enclose a parcel, and pinch together to seal. Make sure the potato filling is nicely sealed in or it will spill out during the next step.

6   Flip the dough-potato ball over so the seal is on the bottom and use a rolling pin to roll it out into an 8-inch circle. Repeat filling and rolling until you have four 8-inch rounds.

7   **COOK THE PARATHA:** Warm a medium skillet over medium-high heat. Once the skillet is thoroughly heated, carefully place a paratha in the pan. Cook for 2 minutes, until the underside starts to brown and blister, then flip. Add 1½ teaspoons of the oil to the surface of the paratha and spread it around with a spoon. Cook for 2 minutes, until the other side is starting to brown and blister, then flip the paratha again. Add 1½ teaspoons of the oil to the top of the paratha, spread it around, and cook until the underside is golden brown with dark brown spots, about 1 minute, then flip again. Cook the other side until golden brown with dark brown spots, no more than 1 minute. Transfer the paratha to a plate. Repeat to cook the remaining parathas. If there is residual flour in the pan, make sure to wipe it out before adding the next paratha.

1   Divide the potato filling and the dough into 4 balls each.

2   Lightly coat each of the dough balls in flour.

3   Roll out each dough ball into a 6-inch circle.

4   Place a ball of potato filling in the center of each dough circle.

5   Pull the edges of the dough circle over the filling.

6   Pinch the dough together at the top to seal in the filling.

7   Make sure the filling is sealed in, then flip the ball over.

8   Roll out each filled ball into an 8-inch round.

9   Repeat until you have four 8-inch rounds.

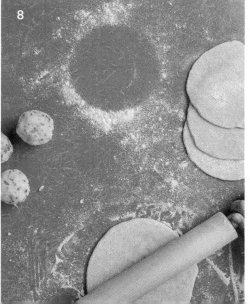

BEANS AND LENTILS

A Beginner's Guide to Making Dal

tip: Insert a long spoon into the pot after the dal comes to a boil to make sure it doesn't boil over while simmering.

1 cup

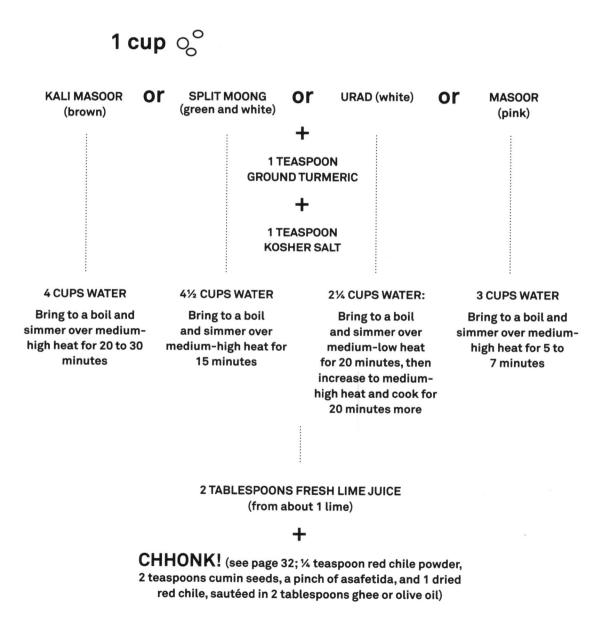

KALI MASOOR (brown) **or** **SPLIT MOONG** (green and white) **or** **URAD** (white) **or** **MASOOR** (pink)

+

1 TEASPOON GROUND TURMERIC

+

1 TEASPOON KOSHER SALT

4 CUPS WATER

Bring to a boil and simmer over medium-high heat for 20 to 30 minutes

4½ CUPS WATER

Bring to a boil and simmer over medium-high heat for 15 minutes

2¼ CUPS WATER:

Bring to a boil and simmer over medium-low heat for 20 minutes, then increase to medium-high heat and cook for 20 minutes more

3 CUPS WATER

Bring to a boil and simmer over medium-high heat for 5 to 7 minutes

2 TABLESPOONS FRESH LIME JUICE (from about 1 lime)

+

CHHONK! (see page 32; ¼ teaspoon red chile powder, 2 teaspoons cumin seeds, a pinch of asafetida, and 1 dried red chile, sautéed in 2 tablespoons ghee or olive oil)

The Most Basic Dal

Serves 4

———

For the dal

1 cup masoor dal (also known as split and dehusked pink lentils, red lentils, or dhuli masoor)

1 teaspoon ground turmeric

1 teaspoon kosher salt

2 tablespoons fresh lime juice (from about 1 lime)

For the seasoning (also known as chhonk)

2 tablespoons ghee or olive oil

2 teaspoons cumin seeds

2 dried red chiles

Pinch of red chile powder

Pinch of asafetida (optional, but really great)

½ cup chopped fresh cilantro (stems and leaves), for garnish

Serve with rice or roti

You'll find this dal as a building block of dinnertime in many North Indian homes. It's a simple soup that cooks quickly and, when served with rice or roti (perhaps with a side of kachumber, page 107), makes for a hearty, complete meal. It's almost a rite of passage for Indian kids to hate eating dal when they are younger, and then to eventually realize as adults that it is truly the superior soup, and way more comforting and complex than they remembered. There are loads of ways my mom makes dal, but this is her ode to the dish in its purest, most elemental form. The key is the chhonk—the ghee-coated chiles and spices tossed in right at the end (see my ode to chhonk on page 32). You'll want to make and add the chhonk *just* before you eat to ensure you'll taste the strongest *ka-pow* of spices and richness.

tip: For added punch, toss in a minced garlic clove when the dal is done cooking, before you add the chhonk.

1 MAKE THE DAL: In a large pot over high heat, combine the lentils, turmeric, salt, and 3 cups water and bring to a boil. Reduce the heat to medium-high, insert a large long-handled spoon into the pot (to break the surface tension and prevent boiling over), and cook with the spoon still inserted until the lentils are soft and a little mushy, 5 to 7 minutes. Remove from the heat, cover, and let sit for 5 minutes. (Alternatively, in an electric multi-cooker like an Instant Pot, combine the lentils, turmeric, salt, and 3 cups water and cook on manual high pressure for 10 minutes, then allow the pressure to release naturally.) Add the lime juice and set aside.

2 MAKE THE SEASONING: In a small pan or butter warmer over medium-high heat, warm the ghee (or oil). Once the ghee melts (or the oil begins to shimmer), add the cumin seeds and cook until they start to sputter and brown, which should take seconds. Immediately remove the pan from the heat and stir in the dried chiles, red chile powder, and asafetida (if using).

3 Add the seasoning to the cooked lentils and mix thoroughly. Garnish with the cilantro before serving.

Priya's Dal

Serves 4

———

For the dal

1 cup whole masoor dal (also known as whole red lentils or brown lentils—they are brown in color)

1 bay leaf

1 teaspoon ground turmeric

1 teaspoon kosher salt

2 tablespoons fresh lime juice (from about 1 lime)

For the seasoning (also known as chhonk)

2 tablespoons ghee or olive oil

2 teaspoons cumin seeds

2 dried red chiles

Pinch of red chile powder

Pinch of asafetida (optional, but really great)

Serve with rice or roti

There's a reason this is called Priya's Dal, and that is because it is the best dal. I know you're not supposed to pick favorites among cookbook recipes, but I'm going to be honest with you: Eating this dal with rice (or roti) brings me the deepest levels of joy. That's because of the naturally creamy, buttery texture of the lentils, and the way they just soak right into the spice mixture. If you have an electric multi-cooker (like an Instant Pot), this is hands-down the best time to bust it out—I made this dal in my Instant Pot, and the lentils turned out so velvety, I literally shed tears of happiness (true story) as I ate them.

1   MAKE THE DAL: Put the lentils in a bowl, add water to fully cover them, and set aside at room temperature to soak for 1 hour. Drain thoroughly. (If using an electric multi-cooker, skip this step.)

2   In a large pot over high heat, combine the lentils, bay leaf, turmeric, salt, and 4 cups water and bring the water to a boil. Reduce the heat to medium-high, give the lentils a stir, and insert a large long-handled spoon into the pot (to break the surface tension and prevent boiling over). Cook with the spoon still inserted until the lentils are soft but still retain their shape and the entire mixture resembles a thick soup, 20 to 30 minutes. Remove from the heat and let sit for 15 minutes. (Alternatively, in an electric multi-cooker like an Instant Pot, combine the dal, bay leaf, turmeric, salt, and 3 cups water and cook on manual high pressure for 20 minutes, then allow the pressure to release naturally.) Add the lime juice and set aside.

3   MAKE THE SEASONING: In a small pan or butter warmer over medium-high heat, warm the ghee (or oil). Once the ghee melts (or the oil begins to shimmer), add the cumin seeds and cook until they start to sputter and brown, which should take seconds. Immediately remove the pan from the heat and stir in the dried chiles, red chile powder, and asafetida (if using).

4   Add the seasoning to the cooked dal and mix thoroughly.

Shortcut Chhole (Chickpea and Tomato Stew)

Serves 4

___

¼ cup olive oil

1 tablespoon cumin seeds

¼ teaspoon fenugreek seeds

1 teaspoon ground turmeric

4 whole cloves

1 small cinnamon stick

1 medium yellow onion, finely diced

1 tablespoon minced fresh ginger

3 medium Roma tomatoes, diced into ½-inch pieces

1 garlic clove, minced

One 16-ounce can chickpeas, drained

2 tablespoons fresh lime juice (from about 1 lime)

¼ cup full-fat plain yogurt

1 teaspoon kosher salt, plus more if needed

½ cup fresh chopped cilantro (stems and leaves), for garnish

Chickpeas are inescapably omnipresent in North Indian cuisine. You'll find them stuffed in samosas; accompanied by bhature, a puffy, stretchy bread; or dressed in onions and yogurt as a street snack. We Krishnas enjoy our chickpeas as a thick, tomato-y stew—but my mom doesn't make it too often, as dry chickpeas take a very long time to cook. Enter: this shortcut recipe, which my mom emailed to me during a particularly cold and sad winter when I was in college. With canned chickpeas, a few strategic whole spices (don't skip the cinnamon stick!), and yogurt to thicken the broth, this stew somehow manages the richness and complexity of a dish that's been cooking for hours. The first time I made this, I had just broken my wrist ice skating and was wearing a cast. The turmeric got all up in the fabric of the sweaty cast, and my hand ended up smelling like burnt garbage for a full month. But for this chhole—it was totally worth it!

1   In a large skillet over medium-high heat, warm the oil. Once the oil begins to shimmer, add the cumin seeds and fenugreek and cook, stirring, until they turn a medium shade of brown, no more than 30 seconds. Add the turmeric, cloves, and cinnamon stick and cook for another minute, until the turmeric has mostly dissolved into the oil and the spices become very fragrant. Toss in the onion and ginger and sauté until the onion is translucent, 3 to 5 minutes. Increase the heat to high, add the tomatoes, and cook until they have fully wilted, 6 to 7 minutes. Add the garlic and cook for 1 minute more.

2   Reduce the heat to medium and add the chickpeas, lime juice, yogurt, and salt. Use a potato masher or the back of a fork to mash the chickpeas slightly so they become incorporated with the sauce (but don't go too crazy—you want to leave the chickpeas relatively intact). Cook, uncovered, until the chickpeas have taken on a soft, baked potato–like texture, 20 to 25 minutes. Taste and adjust the salt if needed. Garnish with the cilantro before serving.

How I Learned to Cook

By Ritu Krishna

Cooking was never my mom's forte. She had other ambitions. She was smart, definitely a feminist of her time. She wanted to study law and become a lawyer, but she married young and got pregnant with me, then my brothers.

Her role at our house was supervisory—she was the one taking care of her parents, making sure the kids were all at home on time. It was my grandmother whose life revolved around cooking. That was what fulfilled her. In the early days, I used to sit in the kitchen and watch her cook. She would give me small jobs like cleaning the cilantro or picking out the stones from the lentils, or I would just observe.

But when I came to America, I didn't have much of a base as far as cooking went. I could make roti very easily because that was something I did at home. I kind of knew how to make potatoes. I sort of bootstrapped myself into cooking. I watched shows with Julia Child, Jacques Pépin, Martin Yan, and I started experimenting. Dal was easy because I had watched my mother make it—it was basic. I tried dumplings, stir-fries, peanut sauce. Sometimes the dishes would turn out horribly. One time my husband, Shailendra's, older brother came over and I made corn timbale. There was way too much salt, and they wasted no time telling me there was something wrong with it.

Every time Shailendra and I went to India, we would stop somewhere in Europe, and then, when we had Priya and Meera and I was working in the airline industry, we went on these bigger tours to different countries and we'd try the various dishes. I remember having briam in Greece, tagine in Morocco, caponata in Sicily. That all really influenced what I made.

What also influenced me was having Priya and Meera tell me that they didn't want to eat Indian food every single day (even though their dad *would* eat Indian food literally every single day if he could . . . along with pizza and spaghetti). So I would come up with these non-Indian dishes where I could still use Indian ingredients, such as spicy noodles or Mexican food. I remember that *Priya* was honestly the most demanding consumer of my food. I was constantly brainstorming: *What else can I make?* I still enjoy experimenting, though now that Meera and Priya are out of the house and it's just me and my husband, I do it much less.

Cooking brings together so many of the things that I enjoy. First is eating well—nutritious food that tastes good and looks good. Second is being adventurous—doing something different. I love trying new fruits and vegetables, and visiting grocery stores when we travel to a new country. All of my interests—wine, entertaining, nice pottery—really exist around cooking.

When I come home from work, where I am managing people and technology, cooking is a way to get my brain to relax. I can forget about all of that and just be creative. Whenever I put together a dinner party, people tell me my food looks like a painting, with all the different colors. It's like creating art! If I didn't have food, I don't know what I would do. I will probably cook for the rest of my life.

Kadhi (Turmeric-Yogurt Soup)

Meet my favorite soup of all time. Kadhi is similar in texture to cream of _____ soup, but with no cream, and better. All you need to make it are yogurt, chickpea flour, and spices. But don't let the simplicity fool you: Kadhi is both deeply comforting and insanely complex in its flavor, like a cozy blanket draped over a hot bowl of white rice. And my mom's recipe, unlike the liquidy, mild versions I've been served at restaurants, is thick, rich, and spice-forward, with a pleasant tanginess at the end. I absolutely love the strong peppercorn flavor in this dish, but if you don't like peppercorns, feel free to nix them or cut the amount in half.

Serves 4

___

1 cup full-fat plain yogurt (see Tip)

¼ cup chickpea flour

1 teaspoon ground turmeric

1 tablespoon + 2 tablespoons ghee or olive oil, divided

½ teaspoon + 1 teaspoon cumin seeds, divided

½ teaspoon black mustard seeds

½ teaspoon fenugreek seeds

5 whole cloves

2 bay leaves

½ teaspoon whole black peppercorns

1 teaspoon kosher salt, plus more if needed

Lime juice (optional, if your yogurt is not that sour)

¼ teaspoon red chile powder

3 dried red chiles

½ teaspoon asafetida (optional, but really great)

Serve with rice

1 In a large (at least 2-cup) measuring cup with a spout (for easy pouring), mix together the yogurt and chickpea flour until smooth and homogeneous. Stir in 1 cup water, followed by the turmeric—the mixture should be a pale yellow color. Set aside.

2 In a very large, deep pot or Dutch oven over medium heat, warm 1 tablespoon of the ghee (or oil). Once the ghee melts (or the oil begins to shimmer), add ½ teaspoon of the cumin seeds, the black mustard seeds, fenugreek, cloves, bay leaves, and peppercorns all at once and cook until you hear the mustard seeds start to pop, 1 to 2 minutes. Reduce the heat to low, add the yogurt–chickpea flour mixture and 3 cups water, and mix well. Add the salt. Taste—the mixture should be tangy, rich, and distinctly flavored by the spices. Adjust with a few drops of lime juice and more salt if needed. Increase the heat to high and cook, stirring continuously (if you stop stirring, the kadhi will curdle), until the mixture comes to a boil. Insert a large long-handled spoon into the pot to prevent it from boiling over and let cook on high for 10 minutes (if at any point it looks like it might boil over, reduce the heat to medium-high for a minute before turning it back up)—the kadhi should become thicker and brighter in color, like a creamy soup.

3 About 5 minutes before the kadhi is done cooking, in a small pan or butter warmer over medium-high heat, warm the remaining 2 tablespoons ghee (or oil). Once the ghee melts (or the oil begins to shimmer), add the remaining 1 teaspoon cumin seeds and cook until it starts to sputter and turn brown, which should take seconds. Immediately remove the pan from the heat and stir in the chile powder, dried chiles, and asafetida (if using).

4 Add the seasoning to the cooked kadhi and stir to combine.

Khichdi

Serves 4

———

For the dal

½ cup split green mung beans

½ cup dry (uncooked) basmati rice

1 bay leaf

1 teaspoon whole black peppercorns

1 teaspoon ground turmeric

1 teaspoon kosher salt

For the seasoning (also known as chhonk)

¼ cup ghee or unsalted butter

2 teaspoons cumin seeds

2 dried red chiles

Pinch of red chile powder

Pinch of asafetida (optional, but really great)

In India, khichdi is associated with two things: sick days and baby food. It's a quintessential, nutritious, one-pot meal of rice and lentils that's easy to make and easy to digest. But like many things in India consumed by small infants and ailing patients (looking at you, turmeric milk), white people in wellness circles have managed to co-opt the dish, acting as if they have unearthed this momentous discovery. They pronounce it *kitch-are-ee* and use words like "detox" and "cleansing" to describe it. So this is me reclaiming khichdi (it's pronounced like *kitch-ree*, with a slight tongue roll on the "r"), with the version my mom has been making for decades. Her secret ingredient is whole black peppercorns, which tenderize in the pot and give the typically one-note dish a bit of depth and kick. Eat it by itself, with a fried egg, cooked up with veggies, or alongside papad (a crispy lentil cracker available at most Indian grocery stores). Just do all us brown people a favor and remember that khichdi was invented by Indians, not L.A. yoga instructors.

1 **MAKE THE DAL:** In a large pot or Dutch oven over high heat, combine the mung beans, rice, bay leaf, peppercorns, turmeric, salt, and 6 cups water and bring to a boil. Reduce the heat to medium, cover, and simmer until the mung beans and rice are fully cooked and the mixture resembles a thick stew, 20 to 25 minutes, scraping down the sides and giving the mixture a stir 15 minutes in. Turn off the heat and let the khichdi sit, covered, while you make the seasoning. (Alternatively, in an electric multi-cooker like an Instant Pot, combine the mung beans, rice, bay leaf, peppercorns, turmeric, salt, and 6 cups water and cook on the rice setting, or on low pressure for 12 minutes, then allow the pressure to release naturally while you make the seasoning.)

2 **MAKE THE SEASONING:** In a small pan or butter warmer over medium-high heat, warm the ghee (or butter). Once the ghee (or butter) melts, add the cumin seeds and cook until they start to sputter and brown, which should take seconds. Immediately remove the pan from the heat and stir in the dried chiles, red chile powder, and asafetida (if using).

3 Add the seasoning to the khichdi and mix thoroughly.

Caramelized Onion Dal

Serves 4

_____

For the dal

1 cup urad dal (also known as split and husked black gram lentils or ivory white lentils; they're white in color)

1 teaspoon kosher salt

1 teaspoon ground turmeric

2 tablespoons fresh lime juice (from about 1 lime)

For the onion

¼ cup olive oil

1 large yellow onion, sliced into thin strips

For the seasoning
(also known as chhonk)

2 tablespoons ghee or olive oil

1 tablespoon cumin seeds

4 dried red chiles

¼ teaspoon red chile powder

¼ teaspoon asafetida (optional, but really great)

This very fancy update of a standard dal goes all the way back to when my mom was a kid in India. She tried it at an aunt's house, and fell in love with the simple addition of sweet, charred onions atop urad dal, a rich, chewy, almost risotto-like variety of lentil (you're gonna love it, trust me). This dish inspires a unique level of mania in people who try it for the first time—the topping is familiar, but the dish still feels very unique. The onions turn dal, typically a simple, everyday staple, into something really luxurious. When caramelized onion dal makes an appearance at a Ritu dinner party, there are never any leftovers. Also, my mom loves to fake complain about how, whenever she makes this dal, people just pick the onions off the top. But you should totally feel free to do that. Like the cheese-coated top layer of a plate of nachos, the ghee-and-chile-doused caramelized onions are objectively the best part.

1 MAKE THE DAL: In a deep medium skillet over high heat, combine the lentils, salt, turmeric, and 2¼ cups water and bring to a boil. Reduce the heat to medium-low, cover, and cook for 20 minutes. Then increase the heat to medium-high and cook for 3 to 7 minutes more, until the lentils are soft and dry and the water has mostly evaporated. Turn the heat off and let the dal sit for 10 minutes. (Alternatively, in an electric multi-cooker like an Instant Pot, combine the lentils, salt, turmeric, and 1½ cups water and cook on manual high pressure for 6 minutes, then allow the pressure to release naturally.) Add the lime juice and set aside.

2 MEANWHILE, MAKE THE ONION: In a large skillet over medium-high heat, warm the oil. Once the oil begins to shimmer, add the onion slices and spread them in an even layer. Cook, stirring every few minutes to prevent burning, until caramelized and dark brown, 8 to 10 minutes. Top the cooked dal with the caramelized onion.

3 MAKE THE SEASONING: In a small pan or butter warmer over medium-high heat, warm the ghee (or oil). Once the ghee melts (or the oil begins to shimmer), add the cumin seeds and cook until they start to sputter and brown, which should take seconds. Immediately remove the pan from the heat and mix in the dried chiles, red chile powder, and asafetida (if using).

4 Top the dal and onions with the seasoning. Don't stir! You're going for a dramatic presentation.

Indian Ribollita

Serves 4 to 6

¼ cup good olive oil, plus more for serving

1 teaspoon whole black peppercorns

2 small Indian green chiles or serrano chiles, finely chopped

1 medium yellow onion, finely diced

1 medium zucchini, diced into ½-inch pieces

2 medium Roma tomatoes, diced into ½-inch pieces

Two 16-ounce cans cannellini or great northern beans, drained

1 tablespoon finely chopped fresh rosemary, plus more for serving

2 garlic cloves, minced

1 teaspoon kosher salt, plus more if needed

1 teaspoon freshly ground black pepper

1 cup (torn ½-inch pieces) stale sourdough bread

Pitted kalamata olives, chopped, for garnish

Shaved or grated Parmesan cheese, for garnish

One of the most memorable meals from the Krishna family travel diary will always be when we dined in a small, old farmhouse in Tuscany, surrounded by animals and (to my dad's chagrin) no bathrooms other than porta-potties. For the first time, we ate the classic Tuscan bean soup ribollita, which features plump white beans, thick pieces of bread, and a fruity slick of olive oil on top. My mom became obsessed with re-creating it at home, but for our slightly spicier tastes. This riff on the soup uses all the familiar ribollita ingredients—cannellini beans, rosemary, garlic—but ups the ante with lots more veggies, a healthy dose of green chiles, and kalamata olives, in addition to the Parmesan and olive oil garnish, to give the soup its briny, funky depths.

> **tip:** Pull out your best olive oil for this recipe—it makes a huge difference.

1   In a large pot or Dutch oven over medium-low heat, warm the oil. Once the oil begins to shimmer, add the peppercorns and chiles. Cook, stirring, for 1 minute, then increase the heat to medium-high and add the onion. Cook until the onion becomes translucent, 5 to 7 minutes. Reduce the heat to medium, add the zucchini and tomatoes, and cook until the zucchini is al dente and still bright green in color, 8 to 10 minutes.

2   Add the beans, rosemary, garlic, salt, ground black pepper, and 4 cups water, increase the heat to high, and bring the soup to a boil. Then reduce the heat to low, mash the beans lightly with a potato masher or a large spoon (just so they soak into the soup—you still want them to keep most of their shape), cover, and cook for 10 minutes. Right at the end of the cooking time, stir in the bread. Taste and adjust the salt if needed (but remember that you'll also be adding olives and cheese, which are both salty).

3   To serve, ladle the soup into individual bowls and garnish with more rosemary, the olives, Parmesan, and a drizzle of olive oil.

Indian-ish English Breakfast Baked Beans

One of the many side effects of the difficult decades of British colonization in India was an exchange of culinary traditions—the popularity of tea time and Cadbury chocolate in India, and of chicken tikka masala in Britain, are just a few results of this cross-pollination. The same goes for sweet, molasses-y Heinz baked beans in tomato sauce, which my family has always loved deeply. Straight out of the teal-colored can, though, the beans are pretty one-note. So my mom doctors them up with ingredients we all love—tomatoes, onions, chiles, and the funky spice blend chaat masala—to give them a lot more character. You can enjoy these beans the classic way—over toast, perhaps with some fried eggs and Caramelized Ginger Mushrooms (page 104)—or do as my brilliant chef friend Clare does and crack a few eggs directly on top of the pan of beans to make an Indian-ish imitation shakshuka!

Serves 4

——

1 tablespoon olive oil

1 teaspoon cumin seeds

½ small yellow onion, finely diced

1 small Indian green chile or serrano chile, finely chopped

2 medium Roma tomatoes, diced into ½-inch pieces

One 14-ounce can vegetarian baked beans (we prefer Heinz)

1 tablespoon chaat masala

2 tablespoons finely chopped fresh cilantro (stems and leaves)

1   In a nonstick medium skillet over medium-high heat, warm the oil. Once the oil begins to shimmer, add the cumin seeds and cook until they turn a medium shade of brown, about 1 minute max. Reduce the heat to medium and add the onion and chile. Spread them in an even layer in the pan and cook until the onion is brown and starts to caramelize, 5 to 7 minutes. Add the tomatoes and sauté until they become soft and resemble a chunky tomato sauce, 2 to 3 minutes. Add the baked beans, chaat masala, and cilantro and mix well.

GRAINS AND NOODLES

Chile Peanut Rice

Just like fried rice makes use of old, crusty rice and whatever stuff you have in your fridge at the moment, this is my mom's way of gussying up leftover basmati rice with *her* kitchen staples. In the case of this particular variation, every ingredient plays its part beautifully: the earthy fried mustard seeds and curry leaves; the mildly sweet, almost-caramelized onions; the crunchy peanuts; and the lingering heat from the chiles. It's a glorious study in balance.

Serves 4

---

3 cups cooked basmati rice (from about 1 cup dry rice; see page 18)

1 teaspoon kosher salt, plus more if needed

2 tablespoons fresh lime juice (from about 1 lime), plus more if needed

¼ cup + ¼ cup ghee or olive oil, divided

1 tablespoon black mustard seeds

10 fresh curry leaves

1 cup roasted unsalted peanuts

2 small Indian green chiles or serrano chiles, halved lengthwise (no need to stem them)

1 medium yellow onion, sliced into thin strips

2 tablespoons chopped fresh cilantro (stems and leaves), for garnish

1 In a large bowl, combine the cooked rice, salt, and lime juice. Set aside.

2 In a shallow medium pan over medium heat, warm ¼ cup of the ghee (or oil). Once the ghee melts (or the oil begins to shimmer), add the black mustard seeds and as soon as they begin to pop and dance around in the oil, which should be within seconds, remove the pan from the heat. Add the curry leaves, making sure they get fully coated in the oil (there may be more popping and splattering, and that's okay!). The leaves should immediately crisp up in the residual heat.

3 Return the pan to medium-low heat and add the peanuts. Cook, stirring, until the peanuts turn a medium shade of brown and become fragrant, 5 to 8 minutes. Pour the peanut-spice-oil mixture over the rice and toss gently to incorporate.

4 In the same pan over medium heat, warm the remaining ¼ cup ghee (or oil). Once the ghee melts (or the oil begins to shimmer), add the chiles and onion, spread them in an even layer in the pan, and cook until the onion is lightly browned and starting to caramelize, 5 to 7 minutes. Stir the sautéed onion and chiles into the rice. Taste and adjust the salt and lime juice if needed. Garnish with the cilantro before serving.

Dalia (Savory Bulgur Wheat Bowl)

Serves 4

2 tablespoons olive oil

1 teaspoon ajwain seeds

3 small Indian green chiles or serrano chiles, halved lengthwise (no need to remove the stems)

1 tablespoon minced fresh ginger

½ cup frozen mixed vegetables (I like those mixed bags of corn, carrots, and peas)

1 cup dry (uncooked) bulgur wheat

1 ½ teaspoons kosher salt, plus more if needed

Bulgur wheat: It ain't just for tabbouleh anymore. But really, am I the only one who doesn't actually love tabbouleh all that much? It tastes like grass, and the teeny bits of parsley always get stuck in my teeth. Here's a far more interesting use for bulgur wheat—my mom's savory take on an Indian breakfast porridge called dalia. Typically dalia is made with jaggery or plain sugar, similar to oatmeal, but my mom discovered that it tastes even better accompanied by sharp, aromatic flavors like ajwain (that oregano-like herb found all over Indian cuisine) and ginger. It's a nourishing, enlivening take on a grain bowl that you can eat at any time of day, and best of all, it requires minimal chopping (frozen veggies, y'all). Dalia is wonderful on its own, but my mom also loves topping it with any kind of chutney or *achar* (pickle) she has on hand (we recommend the Green Chile and Cherry Tomato Pickle, page 64).

1   In a medium pot or Dutch oven over medium-high heat, warm the oil. Once the oil begins to shimmer, add the ajwain seeds and cook until they turn lightly brown, no longer than 1 minute. Turn off the heat and stir in the chiles and ginger.

2   Return the pot to medium-high heat, add the frozen vegetables, and cook for 3 to 5 minutes, until they are somewhat (but not completely) thawed. Add the bulgur wheat, salt, and 2 cups water. Increase the heat to high and bring the water to a gentle boil. Reduce the heat to medium-low, cover, and cook for 15 to 20 minutes, until all the water has been absorbed. Turn off the heat and let the dalia rest, covered, for 10 minutes. Uncover and fluff with a fork. Taste and adjust the salt if needed before serving.

Tomato Rice with Crispy Cheddar

Serves 4

———

2 tablespoons olive oil

1 small yellow onion, finely chopped

1 small Indian green chile or serrano chile, finely chopped

10 medium Roma tomatoes, diced into ½-inch pieces

1 teaspoon kosher salt

3 cups cooked basmati rice (from about 1 cup dry rice; see page 18)

1 cup shredded sharp white cheddar cheese

I could use all sorts of fancy words to explain this dish, but the best description is this: pizza in rice form. The inspiration for the recipe, though, is oddly enough not Italian—it's a hybrid of a classic South Indian tomato rice with onions and a shockingly fantastic Spanish rice recipe my mom and I photocopied out of my seventh-grade Spanish textbook for a school project. The crispy, bubbly, broiled cheddar topping (use the sharpest white cheddar you can find!) adds a little somethin' somethin', making it a worthy dinner party dish. The lovely photographer of this very book, Mackenzie Kelley, called it "even better than pizza" (!!!!).

1   Adjust an oven rack to the highest position and preheat the oven to 500°F.

2   In a large pan over medium-high heat, warm the oil. Once the oil begins to shimmer, add the onion and chile, spread them out in an even layer in the pan, and cook until the onion becomes translucent and starts to lightly char, 5 to 7 minutes.

3   Increase the heat to high and add the tomatoes, using the back of a spoon to lightly crush them. Cook, stirring occasionally, until the tomatoes break down into a chunky sauce, 5 to 6 minutes, then add the salt.

4   Put the cooked rice in an 8-inch square (or similar size) baking dish, then fold in the tomato sauce. (You can also do the folding in a separate bowl and then transfer the rice to the baking dish, if you doubt your ability to not spill rice and sauce everywhere.) Evenly distribute the grated cheese over the top.

5   Switch the oven to broil and place the baking dish on the top oven rack. Broil for about 3 minutes, until the top bubbles and turns golden brown. Serve immediately.

Warm Cumin, Asparagus, Tomato, and Quinoa Salad

This salad follows an easy formula my mom has developed over the years for making a bright, balanced, not-sad desk lunch. Start by sautéing a crunchy vegetable in cumin and olive oil, then add tomatoes, garlic, lime, chiles, and the grain of your choice. She chose asparagus as the star in this recipe because she loves the way it chars and gets this crisp cumin coating in the pan. Quinoa is the base for no other reason than the fact that my dad buys it in overwhelmingly large quantities at Costco . . . and I *do* love its naturally nutty flavor. But you can sub in whatever vegetables and grains you like most. It's the varying textures and colors that are key here.

Serves 2

1 tablespoon + 1 tablespoon olive oil, divided

1 teaspoon cumin seeds

1 pound asparagus, trimmed and cut into 2-inch pieces (about 4 cups)

1½ cups cooked white quinoa (from about ½ cup dry quinoa; see page 19)

1½ cups cherry tomatoes, halved

1 garlic clove, minced

1 teaspoon kosher salt

1 small Indian green chile or serrano chile, finely chopped

1 tablespoon fresh lime juice (from about half a lime)

1   In a large nonstick skillet over medium-high heat, warm 1 tablespoon of the oil. Once the oil begins to shimmer, add the cumin seeds and cook until they turn a medium shade of brown, about 1 minute max. Add the asparagus, cover, and cook for 4 to 6 minutes, until slightly charred but still bright green.

2   In a large bowl, combine the asparagus, cooked quinoa, tomatoes, garlic, salt, and chile. Add the remaining 1 tablespoon oil and gently mix. Just before serving, stir in the lime juice. This salad keeps, covered, at room temperature for up to 1 day, or refrigerated for up to 3 days.

Quinoa Shrimp Pulao

Serves 4

———

3 tablespoons olive oil

1 medium yellow onion, diced into ½-inch pieces

2½ tablespoons minced fresh ginger

2 small serrano chiles, finely chopped

½ teaspoon ground turmeric

4 garlic cloves, minced

1 pound peeled and deveined raw small shrimp

1 medium green bell pepper, diced into ½-inch pieces

1 medium red bell pepper, diced into ½-inch pieces

1 teaspoon kosher salt, plus more if needed

3 cups cooked white quinoa (from about 1 cup dry quinoa; see page 19)

1 tablespoon fresh lime juice (from about half a lime)

⅓ cup chopped fresh cilantro (stems and leaves)

My aunt Sangeeta, pictured below with her husband, Hemant, has two loves: quinoa, and recipes that take less than twenty minutes to make. This dish of hers represents both. Through the years, Sangeeta has experimented with putting quinoa in literally everything—stews, salads, DESSERTS (see Quinoa Kheer, page 199). This dish, a take on pulao (an Indian comfort food of steamed rice and veggies), is her absolute best quinoa creation—good enough even to serve to quinoa cynics (just ask Sangeeta's daughter Meha). The key is cooking the shrimp and veggies on low heat, so the shrimp doesn't get rubbery and the peppers maintain their al dente crunch. File this recipe under "weeknight back-pocket recipes I don't even have to think about."

tip: Sauté the shrimp and vegetables while the quinoa is cooking. Then all you have to do is throw everything together, and you're basically done.

1   In a large Dutch oven over medium-high heat, warm the oil. Once the oil begins to shimmer, add the onion and sauté until translucent, 4 to 6 minutes. Reduce the heat to low and add the ginger, chiles, turmeric, and garlic. Cook, stirring, for 2 minutes, then add the shrimp. Keep stirring for 5 minutes, then add the green and red bell peppers and the salt. Cook for 3 to 4 minutes more, until the shrimp turn light pink and the peppers become slightly soft.

2   Increase the heat to high, add the cooked quinoa, and cook for 2 minutes more, or until the quinoa is fully incorporated and soaked with the seasonings. Add the lime juice and cilantro, then taste and adjust the salt if needed. Turn off the heat and let sit for 15 minutes before serving.

Malaysian Ramen

Serves 2

Two 3-ounce packages chicken-flavored ramen (I use Maruchan, but any of your favorite brands will work)

3 tablespoons vegetable oil

2 garlic cloves, minced

1 teaspoon minced fresh ginger

½ medium red onion, finely diced

1 large carrot, finely diced

2 tablespoons low-sodium soy sauce

1 teaspoon distilled white vinegar

1 teaspoon Sriracha or your favorite Asian chile sauce

3 cups roughly chopped baby spinach (about ½ bunch)

Fresh lime juice

1 tablespoon roasted unsalted peanuts, crushed

What's a cookbook without a fancy take on instant ramen?!?! Mine comes from the Motgi family—Shashi, Guru, and their daughters, Megha and Anjali—who are among our oldest and best friends. We Krishnas and the Motgis spent over a decade traveling around the world together during our school spring breaks, so we treat each other like family. When I was growing up, if I found out that Shashi Aunty's mom, Gowri, who lived in Malaysia, was making this ramen—her quick, kid-friendly version of the noodles sold by street hawkers—there was a 100 percent chance I would be showing up unannounced for dinner. What I love about this dish is that instead of ending up with a noodle soup, you get this semi-cooked, slightly crunchy noodle stir-fry that combines the best parts of munching on dry instant ramen (we all do it!) and eating pan-fried noodles. It's like no amped-up ramen you've ever had before. Also, this recipe is made for tinkering: Add more veggies, throw a runny soft-boiled egg on top, nix the peanuts, spritz on more lime juice . . . Choose your own Malaysian ramen adventure.

1   Break each block of noodles in half. Reserve one packet of seasoning (discard the other or save for something else) and set the noodles and seasoning aside.

2   In a large pan over medium heat, warm the oil. Once the oil begins to shimmer, add the garlic, ginger, onion, and carrot. Cook until the veggies start to soften and the garlic and ginger start to brown, 4 to 5 minutes, then stir in the soy sauce, vinegar, Sriracha, and about ½ teaspoon of the ramen seasoning. Add the spinach, noodles, and ½ cup water, then toss the noodle cakes and veggies in the sauce. When the noodles start to soften (about 4 to 5 minutes), use a large spoon to break them apart and continue tossing them vigorously in the sauce.

3   Reduce the heat to low, cover, and cook until the water has been absorbed and the noodles are leathery and dry, 5 to 7 minutes.

4   Add a generous squeeze of lime juice. Taste and add more lime juice if desired, then sprinkle the peanuts on top.

Rice Noodle Poha

Serves 4 to 6

———

2 tablespoons olive oil

2 teaspoons black mustard seeds

7 fresh curry leaves

2 large russet potatoes, diced into ½-inch pieces

½ small onion, finely diced

1 small Indian green chile or serrano chile, finely chopped

8 ounces thin rice noodles

¼ teaspoon ground turmeric

¾ teaspoon + ½ teaspoon kosher salt, divided, plus more if needed

1 tablespoon granulated sugar

2 tablespoons fresh lime juice (from about 1 lime), plus more if needed, plus lime wedges for serving

½ cup chopped fresh cilantro (stems and leaves), for garnish

Ketchup, for serving (optional)

Cilantro Chutney, for serving (optional; page 62)

Poha is a classic, hearty Indian breakfast dish, made of potatoes, onions, lots of crunchy spices, and a base of flattened rice. But that flattened rice is very temperamental. It dries out easily. It gets mushy. So my aunt Rachna came up with the idea of making poha out of rice noodles, which turns out to be a huge upgrade—they're glassy-looking, chewy, and waaaay easier to cook with. Also, if I had it my way, I would sub in noodles for everything, because noodles are the best, and I would take them over rice any day!!! Let's quickly talk about accompaniments: These noodles taste wonderful on their own, but typically Rachna will serve them with both Cilantro Chutney (page 62) and ketchup, because her daughter, Mitali, cannot live without the former, and her son, Ruchir, cannot live without the latter. Ketchup plus noodles: Trust me on this.

1   In a large, deep skillet over medium-high heat, warm the oil. Once the oil begins to shimmer, add the black mustard seeds and as soon as they begin to pop and dance around in the oil, which should be within seconds, remove the pan from the heat. Add the curry leaves, making sure they get fully coated in the oil (there may be more popping and splattering, and that's okay!). The leaves should immediately crisp up in the residual heat.

2   Return the pan to medium-high heat and add the potatoes, onion, and chile. Sauté until the potatoes start to soften and brown slightly but aren't yet fully cooked, 6 to 7 minutes. Add ½ cup water, reduce the heat to medium, cover, and cook for 8 to 10 minutes more, until the potatoes are soft and fully cooked.

3   Meanwhile, cook the noodles according to the package instructions. Drain, reserving 1 cup of the cooking water, and transfer the noodles to a large bowl.

4   Sprinkle the turmeric, ¾ teaspoon of the salt, and the sugar onto the noodles and toss to combine, using tongs to prevent the noodles from turning into mush. If the noodles are sticking together, add a little bit of the reserved cooking water to make them easier to work with. The noodles should turn a pale yellow color.

5   When the potatoes and onion are done cooking, add the remaining ½ teaspoon salt, then add the noodles, tossing with tongs to combine the noodles and vegetables. Cover and cook over medium-low heat for 2 minutes. Add the lime juice. Taste and adjust the salt and lime if needed. Garnish with the cilantro and serve with lime wedges (and ketchup + Cilantro Chutney, if you want!).

DCC: Dahi Cheeni Chawal (Sweetened Yogurt Rice)

Serves 4

———

3 cups cooked basmati rice (from about 1 cup dry rice; see page 18), cooled to room temperature

1 cup full-fat plain Greek yogurt

3 to 4 tablespoons granulated sugar, depending on your tastes

I wasn't sure if it made sense to put a dish in this book that consists of merely rice, yogurt, and a boatload of sugar, but the truth is, dahi cheeni chawal (in Hindi, *dahi* = yogurt, *cheeni* = sugar, *chawal* = rice) is a Krishna family classic. My mom started making it on Tuesdays (the day of the week when she fasts, which for her means not eating salt), as a simple meal that used the leftover rice from the rest of our family's dinner. But as often happens, my sister and I started sneaking bites of my mom's dahi cheeni chawal, and we fell in love with it, too. We nickname everything in our house (case in point: my parents call me Chhotu, which means "little one" in Hindi, and my sister Golu, meaning "round one"—which is cute but not the most PC), so dahi cheeni chawal was christened "DCC," and my sister ate it every Tuesday until she left for college. There's something about well-cooked rice, tangy yogurt, and the unhinged sweetness of white sugar that will forever be deeply comforting to me.

1   In a large bowl, combine the rice, yogurt, and sugar. That's it!

Sabudana (Peanut-Lime Tapioca)

Serves 4

———

1 cup white tapioca pearls (the small ones, *not* the kind used for bubble tea)

3 tablespoons olive oil

1 tablespoon black mustard seeds

12 fresh curry leaves

4 small Indian green chiles or serrano chiles, halved lengthwise (no need to stem them)

½ cup roasted unsalted peanuts

1 teaspoon kosher salt, plus more if needed

2 tablespoons fresh lime juice (from about 1 lime), plus more if needed, plus lime wedges for serving

1 tablespoon chopped fresh cilantro (stems and leaves), for garnish

It's hard not to love the squishy, mochi-like texture of tapioca pearls. But most people I talk to are only used to seeing them in bubble tea or pudding. I have two words for you: SAVORY. TAPIOCA. Or, as we call it, sabudana, a light, easy-to-eat-a-whole-bowl-of Indian breakfast made up of small white tapioca pearls, peanuts, chiles, spices, and plenty of lime. There are lots of ways to season tapioca, but my mom prefers taking the South Indian route, with oiled-up curry leaves and black mustard seeds, as the crisp texture contrasts nicely with the pillowy bounce of the tapioca. Just be sure you're buying the right kind of tapioca: You're looking for the small white pearls, not the big black ones used in bubble tea. We often eat sabudana with bikaneri bhujia (check out my ode to these fried spicy bits on page 34), but it tastes wonderful all the same topped with oodles of lime juice. Don't forget to plan ahead for the overnight soak of the tapioca.

1   Rinse the tapioca in a fine-mesh sieve to get rid of any starchy powder. In a large bowl, combine the tapioca and 1½ cups water. Cover and set aside at room temperature to soak overnight.

2   In the morning, drain the tapioca. The pearls should be soft enough to squeeze. Set aside.

3   In a large nonstick skillet over medium-high heat, warm the oil. Once the oil begins to shimmer, add the black mustard seeds and as soon as they begin to pop and dance around in the oil, which should be within seconds, remove the pan from the heat. Add the curry leaves, making sure they get fully coated in the oil (there may be more popping and splattering, and that's okay!). The leaves should immediately crisp up in the residual heat.

4   Return the pan to medium heat, add the chiles and peanuts, and cook, stirring continuously to prevent burning, for 2 to 4 minutes, until the peanuts turn slightly brown and emit a strong peanutty fragrance. Add the drained tapioca and mix well—some of the tapioca orbs will become glossy, while others will remain translucent, which is all perfectly okay. Add the salt and lime juice. Remove from the heat, taste, and add more salt and lime juice if needed. Garnish with the cilantro and serve with lime wedges.

ONE CHICKEN AND THREE FISH RECIPES

Garlic-Ginger Chicken with Cilantro and Mint

Serves 4

___

For the marinade

8 garlic cloves, minced

2 tablespoons minced fresh ginger

1 tablespoon finely chopped fresh mint leaves, plus more for garnish

1 tablespoon finely chopped fresh cilantro leaves, plus more for garnish

3 tablespoons olive oil

3 tablespoons fresh lemon juice (from 1 lemon)

1 tablespoon ground coriander (freshly ground is best)

1 teaspoon ground turmeric

½ teaspoon red chile powder

1 teaspoon amchur (dry mango powder)

¾ teaspoon kosher salt

For the chicken

4 boneless, skinless chicken breasts (½ to ¾ pound each)

1 teaspoon olive oil

Many cookbooks come chock-full of chicken recipes. Not this one. There is only one chicken recipe in here because this is the only chicken recipe I need. This chicken, which is the brainchild of my aunt Sonia, is legendary among our cousins. Until I wrote this cookbook, though, no one knew what, exactly, went into it. Whenever my aunt would make it on a family vacation, she'd disappear for a half hour and reemerge with a Ziploc bag filled with the marinade and the chicken breasts. No one (not even her only daughter, Isha) was allowed to know the contents. The marinating chicken would smell so good, I'd legitimately have thoughts about eating it raw, carpaccio-style (which is disgusting, I know!). Well, folks, I am here to tell you that, after much negotiation, I have finally pried that chicken recipe out of Sonia's hands. Both the marinade and the cooking method (low and sort of slow) feel ingenious to me, and the payoff is huge: Charred, spicy, slightly funky, juicy chicken that is equally wonderful by itself or rolled up in a roti, taco-style, and served with various salads and chutneys.

1 **MAKE THE MARINADE:** In a medium bowl, mix the garlic, ginger, mint, cilantro, the 3 tablespoons oil, and lemon juice into a paste.

2 In a small bowl, mix together the coriander, turmeric, red chile powder, amchur, and salt, then add the mixture to the garlic-ginger paste and stir well to combine. Transfer the marinade to a large resealable bag.

3 **MAKE THE CHICKEN:** Place the chicken breasts in the marinade and seal the bag tightly. Use your hands to gently massage the marinade onto the chicken breasts, making sure to evenly coat each breast. Refrigerate the chicken for 2 hours.

4 Warm a large skillet over medium-high heat. Once the pan is quite hot, add the oil, swirling the pan to coat the entire surface. Reduce the heat to medium, remove the chicken from the marinade, and add it to the pan. Cook the breasts for 1 to 2 minutes (without moving them!), until they turn lightly golden on one side, then flip them and cook for 1 to 2 minutes, until they start to become golden on the second side. Reduce the heat to low, cover, and cook the chicken for 10 minutes (without peeking!). Turn off the heat (if you

continued

Garlic-Ginger Chicken with Cilantro and Mint,

continued

have an electric stove, take the pan off the heat) and let the chicken sit, covered, for 10 to 15 minutes, depending on the thickness of the breasts. Don't lift the lid, or you'll release the hot steam that cooks the chicken.

5 Check to make sure the breasts are cooked through—there should not be any pink in the middle and, if you have a meat thermometer, the chicken should register at least 165°F. Place the chicken on a cutting board and slice each breast into strips. Garnish with mint and cilantro.

Kachumber Tilapia

Serves 4

———

For the fish

½ cup fresh lime juice (from about 4 limes)

2 garlic cloves, minced

2 tablespoons minced fresh ginger

2 small Indian green chiles or serrano chiles, finely chopped

1 teaspoon red chile powder

½ teaspoon kosher salt

4 tilapia fillets (½ pound each)

For the kachumber topping

1 Persian cucumber or ½ English cucumber, finely diced

3 medium Roma tomatoes, seeded and finely chopped

1 tablespoon finely chopped fresh cilantro (stems and leaves)

½ teaspoon kosher salt

1 tablespoon fresh lime juice (from about half a lime)

2 tablespoons olive oil, for cooking the fish

When my sister and I left for college, my mom dealt with her empty-nester status by literally moving herself and my father across the world to the Philippines, where she'd been assigned to open a new branch of her company. She packed her suitcases full of wine (this actually happened) and made the big move from Texas to East Asia, where she stayed for almost three years. Filipino cuisine is not the friendliest to vegetarians, so while she was there, she decided to start eating fish. She sourced a few recipes from her fancy friend Shanti, who is from Kerala (the coastal, seafood-loving part of India), and his kachumber tilapia became a regular in her dinner rotation. It's incredibly straightforward, with a simple marinade of ginger, chiles, and garlic and a topping of kachumber, that limey Indian salad I was yammering about on page 107. In addition to being quite healthy yet intensely flavorful, it's also the only fish dish I've ever had that actually reheats really nicely—just keep the kachumber topping separate.

1 MARINATE THE FISH: In a dish that will fit all four fillets, mix together the lime juice, garlic, ginger, green chiles, and red chile powder. Sprinkle the fillets on both sides with the salt, then place the fish in the dish with the marinade, turning each fillet to coat both sides. Cover the dish with plastic wrap and refrigerate for 2 hours.

2 MEANWHILE, MAKE THE KACHUMBER TOPPING: In a medium bowl, combine the cucumber, tomatoes, cilantro, salt, and lime juice. Set aside.

3 COOK THE FISH: In a large nonstick skillet over medium-high heat, warm the oil. Once the oil begins to shimmer, add the fish fillets and the marinade. (If you can't fit all the fillets in the pan at one time, cook them in two batches, using 1 tablespoon of the oil for each.) Cook the fish for 3 to 5 minutes, until the fillets are becoming golden on the underside and the top is starting to flake, then flip and cook for 3 minutes on the second side—again, you should see flaking on top.

4 Serve the fish with the kachumber topping.

Achari Fish

Serves 4

———

½ cup mango achar (pickle) packed in oil (I prefer Mother's Recipe brand—just look at the sugar content on the bottle to make sure it's not a sweet pickle)

4 tilapia fillets (½ pound each)

4 teaspoons + ¼ cup olive oil, divided

Kosher salt

1 large red onion, sliced into thin rings

Achar is a tableside condiment you'll find in many Indian households—it's a combo of fruits and/or vegetables pickled in oil and spices, and it's eaten alongside rice, dal, sabzi, or really anything that could use some salt and complexity. My mom's youngest brother, Sharad, smartly realized that achar and the accompanying spice-infused oil at the bottom of the jar make an excellent marinade for amping up a simple white fish—no measuring or spice blending required. After testing a bunch of different kinds of bottled achars (you can make homemade achar, but honestly, who has the time or patience), he settled on mango for its tangy depths and sweet-and-spicy overtones. But the real genius of this dish comes in cooking rings of red onion in the residual achar oil, then serving them atop the fish—they make for a beautiful, crunchy, slightly charred and caramel-y counterpart. Try these wrapped up in fish tacos! And if you ain't a fish person, you can use the achar marinade on chicken or cauliflower.

tip: Taste the achar before cooking to gauge its saltiness; this will help you determine how much salt to add.

1 Pour the achar (making sure to get some of the oil) into a large resealable bag. Add the fish fillets, seal the bag tightly, and use your hands to gently massage the achar onto the fish, fully coating the fillets. Refrigerate for at least 20 minutes, or up to 2 hours.

2 In a large skillet (one that will fit all 4 fillets) over medium-high heat, warm 4 teaspoons of the oil (if your skillet is too small, you can do this in two batches—just divide the oil). Once the oil begins to shimmer, add the fish fillets and sprinkle the top of each with a small pinch of salt (or to taste; see Tip). Cook the fish for 3 to 5 minutes, until the fillets are golden on the underside and the top is starting to flake, then flip. Sprinkle with a pinch of salt, if desired, and cook for 2 to 3 minutes on the second side—again, you should see flaking on top. Transfer the fish to a plate and return the skillet to the stove.

3 In the same skillet over medium-high heat, warm the remaining ¼ cup oil. Once the oil begins to shimmer, add the onion rings and cook until soft and translucent, 5 to 8 minutes—or longer, if you like them more caramelized.

4 Top the fish with the onion rings.

Orange Peel Fish

A few years ago, my mom's brother Hemant—a fitness fanatic, and an engineer by training—discovered the *en papillote* method of cooking, in which you seal the food in a parchment or foil pouch before baking it in order to retain moisture and flavor. He fell in love with this technique, and putting his analytical mind to work, he experimented with at least twenty different seasoning combinations (RIP, Cheez-It Fish). This one is my all-time favorite, because it's ridiculously simple. The main ingredient is the chopped-up peel of a single clementine—or as Hemant calls the fruit, a "virtually zero-calorie snack"—but that single peel lends an insane amount of texture and aroma to the fish, without any of the bitterness. Hemant loves using sea bass, because it's thick and buttery, but it *is* expensive. I feel strongly that this is a worthwhile splurge (and if you buy it frozen, it's not *so* outrageous), but feel free to use the white fish of your choice, like cod or haddock.

Serves 4

---

4 sea bass fillets (½ pound each)

1 tablespoon olive oil

5 garlic cloves, minced

2 tablespoons minced fresh ginger

½ teaspoon ground turmeric

1 small serrano chile, finely chopped

1 teaspoon kosher salt

Peel of 1 small clementine, finely chopped

Lime wedges, for serving

1 Place the fish on a paper towel and pat dry.

2 In a small bowl, stir together the oil, garlic, ginger, turmeric, chile, and salt into a paste. Using half the paste, coat one side of each fillet.

3 Spread a 2-foot sheet of foil out on the counter. Place all the fish fillets on one half of the foil, paste-side down. Coat the other side of the fillets with the remaining paste, making sure to evenly cover the entire surface area of the fish. Evenly sprinkle the clementine peel over the top of each fillet. Fold the other half of the foil over the fish, then fold each side over three times to seal the foil into a pouch. Refrigerate the pouch for 30 minutes.

4 Preheat the oven to 450°F.

5 Transfer the pouch to a baking sheet and bake for 10 to 14 minutes, depending on the thickness of your fillets, then turn off the oven and let the fish sit in the oven for 1 minute more—the pouch should have puffed up at this point.

6 Remove the baking sheet from the oven and let the pouch cool down for a minute, then unseal the sides of the pouch (be careful of the hot steam inside!). Serve each fillet with a lime wedge for spritzing, and spoon the juices from the foil pouch over the top.

DESSERTS

Shrikhand (Sweet Cardamom Yogurt)

Serves 4 to 6

———

4 cups full-fat plain Greek yogurt (1 quart-size container)

¼ teaspoon + ¼ teaspoon saffron threads

½ cup granulated sugar

Seeds from 4 green cardamom pods, crushed into a powder, or 1 teaspoon ground cardamom (freshly ground is best)

For all the people out there who believe that yogurt could never, ever be a decadent dessert, I present to you the exception to the rule: shrikhand, one of my favorite sweets of all time. It's an impossibly creamy, saffron-studded, I-can't-believe-I-made-this-with-yogurt treat that's typical of the Indian region of Gujarat. My mom started making it because my dad's older brother, Pradeep, loves it. And then my sister and I tried it once and were like, "Okay, yep, here for this," because shrikhand is impossible not to adore. My mom usually makes this with my dad's homemade yogurt (page 43), but you can get that same super-silky texture with good-quality store-bought Greek yogurt. My friend Khushbu came up with the idea of putting shrikhand in a graham cracker pie shell and refrigerating it—I haven't personally tried this, but I imagine it would yield the best no-bake pie ever.

1   Line a large colander with coffee filters or paper towels, overlapping them so that they cover the sides, and set it over a deep plate or bowl. Pour in the yogurt and refrigerate overnight or for up to 12 hours to allow the whey to drain out and thicken the yogurt. In the morning, the yogurt should be very thick—like an even creamier, richer Greek yogurt.

2   Using a mortar and pestle, crush ¼ teaspoon of the saffron threads into a powder.

3   In a large bowl, combine the strained yogurt, sugar, cardamom, and crushed saffron. Mix well—the yogurt should turn a pale yellow color. Top with the remaining ¼ teaspoon whole saffron threads (don't mix, as you want that stained effect) and refrigerate for at least 2 to 3 hours (and up to 8 hours) before serving.

Quinoa Kheer

Serves 4 to 6

___

½ gallon (2 quarts) whole milk

½ cup dry (uncooked) white quinoa, rinsed and drained

½ cup granulated sugar

Seeds from 5 green cardamom pods, crushed into a powder, or 1¼ teaspoons ground cardamom (freshly ground is best)

2 tablespoons roughly chopped unsalted pistachios, for garnish

At this point in the book, you're probably like, "Seriously, you're going to put quinoa in *another* dish? In a *dessert*, of all things? IS NOTHING SACRED ANYMORE?"

I promise I wouldn't force you to put quinoa in a dessert unless I knew it was going to taste insanely good. And this quinoa kheer is truly the best. I was very skeptical when my aunt Sangeeta (a devout quinoa fan) told me that her mom made a version of kheer, a cardamom rice pudding, with quinoa instead of rice. But I asked Sangeeta's mom for the recipe anyway. Her response: "Just make kheer, and use quinoa instead!" (Very helpful.) The end result tastes like a luxurious, cardamom-laced chia pudding, but without that weird chia sliminess. The quinoa grains turn soft and silky, adding a hint of nuttiness to the kheer. They also do an even better job than rice of soaking up the cardamom flavor. Start to finish, this takes about as long as an episode of TV to make, so now you have something to do while you stir! Kheer can be eaten warm or cold, but I like it straight out of the fridge, as it has more thickness and body when chilled.

1 Evenly coat the bottom of a large pot or Dutch oven with 2 table-spoons water (this will prevent the milk from sticking to the bottom of the pot). Pour the milk into the pot and bring it to a boil over high heat. Watch the milk very closely—*as soon as* you start to see bubbles forming, reduce the heat to low (otherwise, the milk will boil over!).

2 Add the quinoa. Increase the heat to medium and cook, stirring continuously, for 15 minutes, then increase the heat to medium-high and cook, stirring continuously, for 30 to 35 minutes more, until the milk resembles heavy cream (it should be thick enough to coat the back of a spoon) and the quinoa is fully cooked. Don't worry if there still seems to be a lot of milk left—it'll soak into the quinoa as the kheer cools.

3 Stir in the sugar and cardamom and let the kheer cool to room temperature. Transfer to a bowl, cover with plastic wrap, and refrigerate overnight or for up to 12 hours—it should resemble a loose rice pudding. When you're ready to serve the kheer, garnish with the pistachios.

Shahi Toast (Cardamom Bread Pudding)

Serves 4 to 6

―――

2 cups heavy cream

6 tablespoons granulated sugar

Seeds from 4 green cardamom pods, crushed into a powder, or 1 teaspoon ground cardamom (freshly ground is best)

2 tablespoons vegetable oil

5 slices white bread, crusts removed, each slice cut into 4 squares

2 tablespoons roughly chopped pistachios, for garnish

Back when my mom was in her teenage years and her kitchen in India was much less amply stocked, she would make a dessert called shahi toast, a bread pudding–esque dish of panfried white bread soaked in cardamom-flavored cream until the bread bits turn drippy, supple, and sweet. It quickly became a favorite of her brother Hemant's, and she'd make it for him when he'd visit from engineering school. My mom forgot about this recipe for a long time, until a few Christmases ago, when she snuck out to buy white bread (Mom buying white bread: Our first clue that something was up) and clandestinely prepared it to surprise Hemant for the holidays. It was pretty adorable seeing his face light up when my mom presented him with shahi toast—like they were both back to being teens in India. Safe to say, the rest of us fell in love with shahi toast that night, too.

1 Coat the bottom of a medium pot or small Dutch oven with 2 tablespoons water (this will prevent the cream from sticking when you heat it), then add the cream. Cook over medium heat, stirring continuously, until the cream is warmed through, 4 to 6 minutes. Turn off the heat and stir in the sugar and cardamom, making sure the sugar has dissolved completely. Set aside.

2 In a large skillet over medium-high heat, warm the oil. Once the oil begins to shimmer, reduce the heat to medium-low, add the bread, and cook until the undersides are golden brown, 4 to 6 minutes. Flip and cook until the other sides have also turned golden brown, 4 to 6 minutes more.

3 In a 9-inch square baking dish, arrange the pieces of bread in a single layer. Give the cardamom cream a stir to fully incorporate the sugar and cardamom, then pour the cream over the bread, making sure each piece of bread is fully soaked with cream.

4 Cover the dish with plastic wrap and refrigerate overnight or for up to 12 hours. Just before serving, garnish with the pistachios.

Boozy Strawberries

Serves 4 to 6

1 pound strawberries, quartered

¼ cup Cointreau or other triple sec (just not the really cheap stuff)

1 teaspoon orange zest

1 tablespoon granulated sugar, plus more if your strawberries aren't very sweet

Putting booze and sugar on fruit is a really easy way to (1) impress your party guests and (2) salvage sub-ideal fruit. Taking inspiration from her love of booze-infused jams, my mom came up with this dressed-up strawberry dessert, and it quickly became one of her great triumphs in flavor pairings: the sugar and the Cointreau (my mom's preferred brand of triple sec) work as amplifiers for the sweet, tangy flavors of the strawberries, and the touch of orange zest freshens everything up. Eat the strawberries by themselves—as my sister and I did as kids, probably getting unknowingly tipsy in the process—or do as my dad would do and spoon them over good-quality vanilla ice cream (for us Texans, that means Blue Bell or bust).

1   In a large bowl, combine all the ingredients. Taste and add more sugar, if needed, keeping in mind that the strawberries will get a shade sweeter as they macerate. Cover and refrigerate for 30 minutes.

2   Serve immediately—don't leave the strawberries in the fridge for much longer, or they'll get too soft.

Eggless Pineapple Cake

A peculiar aspect of bakeries in India is that most of the cakes and pastries sold don't have eggs in them, mainly due to the fact that most traditional Indian desserts don't contain eggs, and for much of the vegetarian population, eggs are considered, as people derisively say, "non-veg." As a result, the most popular cake destination among the enormous Indian community in my hometown of Dallas is an eggless bakery called Hot Breads, and its absolute best dessert is this pineapple cake. PERHAPS YOU ARE SKEPTICAL. *A pineapple cake . . . with no eggs . . . and tofu . . . that's not a pineapple upside-down cake?* Think of this version (which I adapted in turn from the blog *Madhuram's Eggless Cooking*) as more like a light, angel food–esque confection with whipped cream frosting and a mildly acidic but pleasant kick. It's wonderful in its airiness and simplicity—not the kind of cake that will weigh you down.

Serves 12 to 15

For the cake

1 stick (8 tablespoons) unsalted butter, at room temperature, plus more for greasing

½ cup full-fat plain yogurt

½ cup pureed silken tofu (4 ounces)

¼ cup whole milk

2½ cups cake flour

2 teaspoons baking powder

1 teaspoon baking soda

½ teaspoon kosher salt

1¼ cups granulated sugar

2½ cups (two 14-ounce cans) canned diced pineapple, juices drained and reserved

For the frosting

2 cups heavy cream

¼ cup granulated sugar

1   MAKE THE CAKE: Preheat the oven to 350°F. Line a 9 x 13-inch baking pan with parchment paper and grease the parchment with butter.

2   In a medium bowl, stir together the yogurt, tofu, and milk with a wooden spoon until the mixture looks homogeneous. Set aside.

3   In a separate medium bowl, sift together the cake flour, baking powder, baking soda, and salt and set aside.

4   In the bowl of a stand mixer fitted with the paddle attachment, cream the butter and sugar on high speed until light and smooth, about 1 minute. With the mixer running on high, add the yogurt mixture in three additions, beating for about 45 seconds after each. Reduce the mixer speed to low and slowly add the dry ingredients. Mix just until incorporated. Fold in ½ cup of the pineapple chunks with a spatula.

5   Pour the batter into the prepared pan, spreading it evenly and making sure the pineapple is uniformly distributed. Bake for 21 to 23 minutes, until a toothpick inserted into the center of the cake comes out clean. Let the cake cool while you make the frosting.

continued

Eggless Pineapple Cake, continued

6 MAKE THE FROSTING: In the bowl of a stand mixer fitted with the whisk attachment, combine the cream, sugar, and 1 teaspoon of the reserved pineapple juice. Mix on high speed until stiff peaks form, about 2 minutes.

7 Once the cake has cooled *completely*, remove it from the pan and slice it in half lengthwise. Dust off the excess crumbs and brush the edges and crumb sides of the cake halves with the reserved pineapple juice (this will help the cake stay moist).

8 ASSEMBLE THE CAKE: Place one cake layer on a serving platter with the crumb side facing up. Spread the remaining 2 cups pineapple chunks (reserving a couple spoonfuls for garnish) on top of the cake, then spread half the frosting over the pineapple. Set the second cake layer on top, this time with the crumb side facing down. Frost the top and sides of the cake with the remaining frosting and scatter on the reserved pineapple chunks. This cake keeps, refrigerated, for up to 3 to 4 days, after which it will sadly get very dry. Enjoy it quickly!

Anvita's Dump Cake

Serves 8 to 10

──────

One 20-ounce can crushed pineapple in juice

One 21-ounce can cherry pie filling

One 15- or 16-ounce box yellow cake mix

1 stick (8 tablespoons) salted butter, chilled and sliced into small (½-tablespoon) pieces

1 cup chopped pecans

You're probably wondering, *Why, in this book of pseudo-Indian food, is there a recipe for a 1940s-era American dessert? Also, who the heck is Anvita?* The recipe is in here because it's one of those dead-simple desserts with an insanely low effort-to-taste ratio, and Anvita is the wonderful daughter of my grandmother's brother (lol, Indian families) who first made it for me. Dump cakes are truly as straightforward to make as they sound—layer butter, canned fruit, cake mix, and nuts; bake; serve with ice cream (vanilla is the best)—and they were always a hit when my cousin Hirsh and I would visit Anvita in Ann Arbor. Generally I don't much care for canned cherry pie filling, or artificial-tasting pineapple, or even pecans, for that matter—but somehow, in this recipe, the ingredients come together to create this crumbly, fruity, strangely delicious alchemy. It's not even worth questioning, because there's not a single party I've brought this to where I haven't returned home with an empty dish.

1 Preheat the oven to 350°F.

2 Spread the crushed pineapple and its juice over the bottom of an 9 x 13-inch baking dish. Pour the cherry pie filling evenly across the top, keeping the layers distinct. Sprinkle the cake mix over the cherry pie filling, breaking up any lumps with a spoon. Lay the butter slices evenly across the top, followed by the pecans.

3 Bake until the top turns golden brown, about 1 hour. Serve immediately.

DRINKS

Cardamom Chai

Serves 4

———

4 cardamom pods, crushed with the skin still on

4 English Breakfast tea bags

½ cup whole milk, warmed, plus more if needed

4 teaspoons granulated sugar, plus more if needed

Can I rant for just one quick sec? There are few things that annoy me more than when people say "chai tea." Let me set the record straight: *Chai* means "tea" in Hindi. So when you say "chai tea," you are saying "tea tea." JUST CALL IT CHAI.

Now that we have that out of the way: Chai is everything to my mother. She, like many Indians, drinks it every day, sometimes multiple times a day, usually alongside a rusk (a crunchy, toast-like biscuit) or Parle-G biscuits (Indians' go-to cookie for chai dunking). It's her moment to breathe—when she returns from her walk, when we've just finished a big shopping trip, when she's helping her nagging daughter (me) test recipes for a cookbook but wants to take a second between coming home from work and starting to cook. The basic formula for chai of any kind is simple: black tea, milk, and whole spices (typically some combo of cinnamon, cardamom, nutmeg, and ginger). Every person has her own spice blend preference, but the end effect is the same: a warming, aromatic drink that's a nice step up from the usual cup of tea or coffee. Mom's chai is quite straightforward—the only flavoring is cardamom, mostly because she loves cardamom and doesn't think her chai needs much else (I agree). The trick is starting with whole cardamom pods, so the tea really gets infused with that heady, sweetish flavor.

1   In a medium pot over high heat, bring 4 cups water to a boil. Add the cardamom and boil for 1 minute. Add the tea bags and turn off the heat. Cover and let steep for 4 minutes—the tea will become almost black in color. Add the milk and sugar. Taste and adjust the milk and/or sugar if needed.

2   Discard the tea bags and use a tea strainer or fine-mesh sieve to strain the chai into four individual cups.

Ginger-Pepper Chai

This version of chai is kind of like a chai-PLUS—and by that I mean, when you have a sore throat, or it's –15 degrees outside, this chai is your ringer. Soothing, slightly sweet, and all kinds of kicked up from the ginger and black pepper (freshly ground, please!), it works even better for me than cough syrup.

tip: If you want a stronger ginger flavor, pound the minced ginger on a cutting board with the back of a knife to release the juices before adding it to the chai.

Serves 4

2 tablespoons minced fresh ginger

4 English Breakfast tea bags

1 teaspoon freshly ground black pepper

½ cup whole milk, warmed, plus more if needed

4 teaspoons granulated sugar, plus more if needed

1   In a medium pot over high heat, bring 4 cups water to a boil. Add the ginger and boil for 2 to 3 minutes. Add the tea bags and turn off the heat. Cover and let steep for 4 minutes—the tea will become almost black in color. Stir in the pepper, followed by the milk and sugar. Taste and adjust the milk and/or sugar if needed.

2   Discard the tea bags and use a tea strainer or fine-mesh sieve to strain the chai into four individual cups.

South Indian Yogurt Cooler

Serves 4

———

1½ cups full-fat plain yogurt (don't use Greek, as you want a slightly liquidy consistency)

2 tablespoons chopped fresh cilantro (stems and leaves)

4 fresh curry leaves

1 teaspoon minced fresh ginger

1 small Indian green chile or serrano chile, finely chopped

Pinch of asafetida (optional, but really great)

¼ teaspoon kosher salt

¼ cup ice cubes

A few years ago, in an effort to socialize healthfully, my mom and her friends founded a walking group. Every weekend, they wake up at the crack of dawn and traverse one of the three not-totally-flat hiking routes in Dallas. It's the ideal activity for them: They get to meet their step count while also gossiping about Such-and-such Aunty's son's new girlfriend or passing judgment on the bride's sari at the wedding they'd attended the previous night. Instead of Gatorade or green juice or Smartwater or any other fancy workout libations, my mom and her friends cool down with this salted, spiced yogurt drink. In India, salty yogurt is a standard drink on hot summer afternoons—creamy and cooling at the same time. My mom's take (inspired by her friend Jayeshree, a member of the group) is similarly refreshing, with an added kick from bright herbs and ginger. Leave out the chile if you're spice averse—you can really taste it in here.

1   In a blender, combine all the ingredients except the ice. Blend until the mixture looks homogeneous. Add the ice cubes and blend until they are broken down and well integrated but you can still see a few small granules. Serve immediately.

Shikanji (Indian Gatorade)

Serves 4

———

¾ cup fresh lime juice (from about 6 limes)

¾ teaspoon freshly ground black pepper, plus more for serving

¼ cup granulated sugar

1 teaspoon kosher salt

1 cup ice cubes, plus more for serving

Think of this like limeade with a very satisfying curveball. Shikanji is the standard summertime drink that my mom's family in India used to serve guests in lieu of soda (which was usually too expensive). Salt and pepper may not seem like the most obvious ingredients in a warm-weather beverage, but they add this indescribable addictiveness and lip-smacking tang that's similar to the salty, energizing electrolytes in Gatorade—in fact, my dad literally calls this drink "Indian Gatorade." Shikanji also happens to make a great base for a cocktail—add tequila, and you've got yourself an *Indian-ish* margarita (just ask David, my brother-in-law and our family's official drinks guy). And yes, your arms will probably be sore from squeezing all those limes (roll the heck out of them before you squeeze them to maximize the juice). But the wildly refreshing payoff is totally worth it.

1   Combine all the ingredients in a blender with 2 cups water. Blend until everything is fully incorporated and a thin layer of foam forms on the top.

2   Fill four glasses with ice and pour the shikanji over the top, stirring with a spoon just before serving so the pepper is integrated throughout. Garnish each glass with one more tiny pinch of pepper.

Sweet Lassi

———

2 cups full-fat plain yogurt (not Greek, as you want a liquid consistency)

½ cup granulated sugar

1½ cups ice cubes

When I was growing up, there were no smoothies, or juices, or milk shakes in our house. There was just lassi—a sweet, refreshing concoction of yogurt, ice, and sugar. At restaurants, you'll find all kinds of fruit-filled variations, with strawberries, papaya, and the ever-popular mango—but we Krishnas are purists. That's because on hot days, there's nothing like the elemental comfort of icy yogurt and sugar with a foamy top. Some versions of lassi that I've tried are too much ice and not enough yogurt, but this version lets the creaminess and tanginess of the yogurt shine. If there were ever a recipe to splurge on a good brand of yogurt (or make your own—page 43!), this would be it.

1 In a blender, combine the yogurt and sugar and blend until well incorporated. Add the ice cubes and blend again until they are broken up and well integrated with the yogurt and sugar. Serve immediately.

Ritu's Handy Guide to Pairing Wine and Indian Food

The following white wines are best with lighter dishes such as salads, rice dishes, fish, Roti Pizza (page 130), Roti Noodle Stir-Fry (page 133), and appetizers such as Black Pepper and Chile Baked Goat Cheese (page 57) and Lima Bean and Basil Dip (page 52).

- **Drumheller Chardonnay 2016**
  Columbia Valley, Washington State
  A great find! Fruity nose with pear, peach, and pineapple aromas; oaky, balanced, and full-bodied.

- **Chateau de Thauvenay Sancerre 2015**
  Loire Valley, France
  A little fruity with a lovely citrusy bouquet; full-bodied.

- **Italo Cescon Pinot Grigio 2016**
  Veneto, Italy
  Delicate white wine with pear, apple, and citrus notes; light-bodied.

- **Sterling Sauvignon Blanc 2011**
  Napa Valley, California
  Gorgeous flavors of zesty lime, grapefruit, and melon; medium-bodied.

- **La Crema Chardonnay 2012**
  Sonoma Valley, California
  Clean and bright with vanilla notes; buttery, oaky, and full-bodied.

The following red wines are best with more robust dishes such as Matar Paneer (page 70), Aloo Paratha (page 145), Shortcut Chhole (page 153), Indian Ribollita (page 163), Lotus Root and Jammy Tomatoes (page 79), White Bean–Stuffed Poblanos (page 73), and Spinach and Feta Cooked Like Saag Paneer (page 83).

- **Robert Mondavi Cabernet Sauvignon 2009**
  Napa Valley, California
  Ripe and fruity with typical Cab characteristics of mocha, blackberry, and black pepper; rich finish; full-bodied.

- **Sonria Shea Vineyard Pinot Noir 2011**
  Willamette Valley, Oregon
  Fragrant strawberry and cherry bouquet with oak; complex and luscious; medium-bodied.

- **Franciscan Cabernet Sauvignon 2013**
  Napa Valley, California
  One of my go-to wines. Perfumes of chocolate and blackberry; smooth, well-balanced, and full-bodied.

- **Altos Ibericos Reserva Rioja 2012**
  Spain
  I love Rioja wines. Blackberries, cherries, and fig nose; a long finish and full-bodied.

- **Dona Paula Estate Malbec 2016**
  Tupungato, Argentina
  We love Malbecs! Fragrance of plump, dark berries; well-balanced, not too many tannins; full-bodied.

- **Verrazzano Chianti Classico Riserva 2013**
  Italy
  Nose of ripe red fruit followed by notes of tobacco; well blended tannins; medium-bodied.

- **Baldacci Elizabeth Pinot Noir 2012**
  Napa Valley, California
  Very elegant—a bit of a splurge—with a lovely floral bouquet and creamy finish; medium-bodied.

- **Zuccardi Malbec 2014**
  La Consulta, Argentina
  Exquisite fragrance of luscious fruits such as blueberry, with herby notes; full-bodied.

- **Vecchia Cantina Vino Nobile di Montepulciano Poggio Stella 2011**
  Toscana, Italy
  Elegant nose of blueberries and mocha; flavors of old and mature dark fruit; full-bodied.

- **Luca Bosio Barolo 2010**
  Piedmont, Italy
  Fruit-forward, with complex flavors and aromas of dark fruits, truffles, and tobacco; high in tannins; full-bodied.

- **Concha y Toro Gran Reserva Serie Riberas Malbec 2011**
  Santiago, Chile
  Affordable and a good value. A wine with gravitas, with hints of dark fruits; full-bodied.

- **Quilceda Creek CVR Red 2011**
  Columbia Valley, Washington
  If you want to splurge, this is the wine to splurge on. A big, bold wine that will remind you of rich dark chocolate and everything luscious. A long finish; full-bodied.

- **Groom Shiraz 2004**
  Barossa Valley, Australia
  Another wine to splurge on. Bouquet of fresh red berries and a bit of herbs and spices, with subtle oak and bright fruit; extremely full-bodied.

- **Norton Reserva Malbec 2012**
  Lujan de Cuyo, Argentina
  Another go-to wine for our family. Aromas of rich, plump fruits with a velvety finish; full-bodied.

- **Daou Cabernet Sauvignon 2016**
  Paso Robles, California
  With nose of chocolate, coffee, and leather; excellent finish; full-bodied.

- **Rodney Strong Cabernet Sauvignon, All Years**
  Sonoma County, California
  Fragrance of dark berries and some plum. Robust, complex, and full-bodied. Always reliably good.

- **Conundrum Red Blend 2015**
  Napa Valley, California
  Lovely, luscious, and velvety with a bouquet of mature dark berries and cigar; full-bodied.

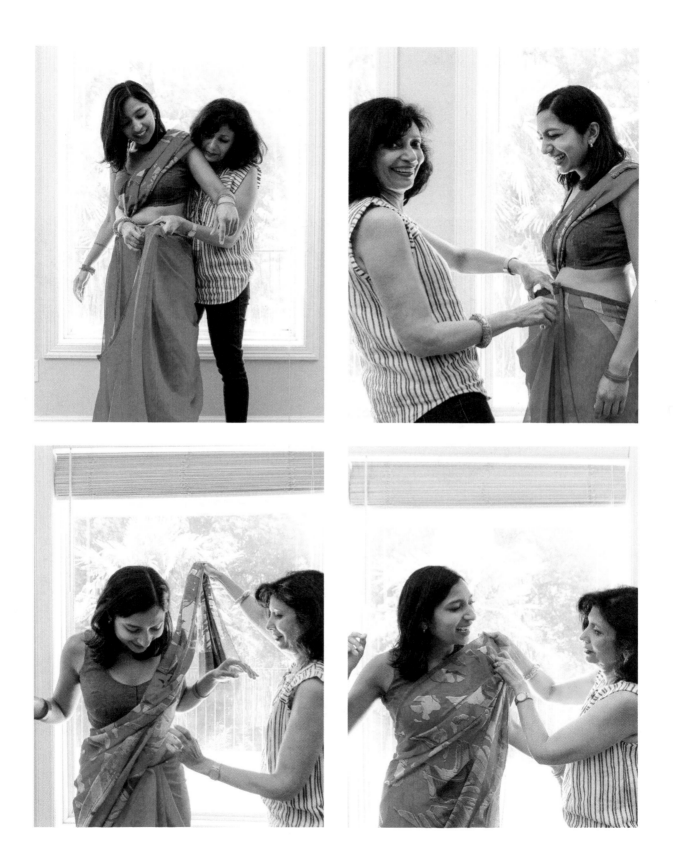

Acknowledgments

This book would not exist without my family. Specifically, my **mom**—who, in addition to her demanding job, dedicated over a year to writing recipes, helping me test them, and having her picture taken while making them; she essentially project managed this cookbook, and is every bit as incredible as she comes across in its pages. And my **dad**, who does the not-so-glamorous job of helping me sort out my finances and, while I was home testing and shooting recipes, washed countless dishes caked in turmeric and cumin. As one of my all-time favorite Bollywood directors, Karan Johar, once said, "It's all about loving your parents." Mom and Dad, I do not take you for granted. I'm insanely lucky.

This family thank-you also extends to my sister, **Meera Krishna**, and my brother-in-law, **David Peterson**, who flew to Dallas just to be a part of the cookbook photo shoot and tested tons of recipes. And also **Gaboo Mama, Sangeeta Mami, Pintoo Mama, Sonia Mami, Atul Mama, Rachna Mami,** and the **Cousin Club,** who also tested recipes and moved around their schedules so that we could photograph them pretending to laugh while eating aloo gobhi.

The first non-family member I want to call out is **Caitlin Ardrey**. People reading this: Caitlin is the definition of a ride-or-die friend. This girl flew to Dallas when I was in the most panicked stage of writing, chopped vegetables, did the dishes, and drove me to the nearest park when I was having one of many breakdowns about whether this book was any good. May we all have friends like Caitlin. Then there's **Lauren Vespoli** and **Kate Taylor**, the greatest roommates, friends, and listeners I could have asked for during the book process. **James Lee:** I want to thank you for just generally being the most supportive. I wish every friend were like you, Jamesy. And **Kelly Tropin**, who will always take my anxiety calls from her car.

The Sambar Squad—Sonia Chopra, Tejal Rao, Khushbu Shah: For being the biggest cheerleaders of this project when I needed it the most, and for giving me a family away from my family. An extra hug to Sonia, who gave my book a much-needed read-through before it went to layout. **Aralyn Beaumont**, who carefully and thoughtfully went through each of my recipes with a fine-tooth comb. **Max Falkowitz:** For your editing help, and for always encouraging me to let my weird side thrive. **Ligaya Mishan:** For being the best, generally. Your pep talks and writing inspire me on a constant basis. **Kerry Diamond:** For being the sagest of sages, and for responding to that one email I sent to info@cherrybombe.com back in 2013. **Chitra Agrawal, Samin Nosrat, Julia Turshen, Ali Rosen, Mary-Frances Heck, Alison Roman:** Folks who offered me guidance on recipe writing and testing (things I hadn't really done before this book), and just calmed my nerves about this whole process in general. And **Padma Lakshmi**—an unbelievable mentor to me and a role model to all women.

Rica Allanic, for coming up with the idea for this book in the first place, and **Sarah Smith**, my agent, for helping me shape it and sell it for big bucks!!!! **The whole team at Houghton Mifflin Harcourt, and particularly my editor, Stephanie Fletcher**, for betting on a book about a weirdo and her family.

My photo shoot dream team: photographer **Mackenzie Kelley**, food stylist **Judy Kim**, and lighting/tech pros **Lauren Vied Allen** and **Jason Kelley**—you brought *Indian-ish* to life in the most spectacular way, and went so, so, so far above and beyond. You all have a standing chai invitation at the Krishna house for life.

The *Hamilton* soundtrack: For giving me my first actually productive writing day on this cookbook, and for reminding me to be patient and WAIT FOR IT.

Think Coffee on Mercer Street: I'm so sorry for buying one coffee and camping out at your shop to write my book for hours; I will try to do better next year.

You, whoever you are: For purchasing this book, or acquiring it by whatever means you ended up with it!!!!! And for taking the time to read the acknowledgments. Wow, what commitment!

The Haters: The school bullies, the people who told me I was bad at my job, and general meanies. I took all those tough times and turned them into a writing career! Also, if you're reading this, I can't believe you purchased my book! That's pretty cool.

Seth Byrum: I hit the jackpot with you, Seb. I don't just love you, I adore you. You proofread my stories, you bake me pies, you let me perform my one-woman show of *Chicago* for you in our living room, and you make me a better person every single day. You don't realize quite how special you are, but that's okay, because I do. What would I do without you?

And lastly, an enormous thank-you to each and every single person who tested a recipe for this book:

Alex Beggs
Ali Rosen
Allie Misch
Amy and Adam Krefman
Angie Yang
Anjali Adukia and Rick Hornbeck
Anjali Motgi
Anna "Lytics" Litman
Anna Polonsky
Aralyn Beaumont
Aurelia Solomon
Avantika Banerjee
Beth Anis
Brittany Geeta Johnson
Brittany Rasansky
Caitlin Ardrey
Camila Hernandez
Camryn Mothersbaugh and Walter Green
Caroline Lange
Carolyn Gaut Kraska
Casey Brown
Clare de Boer
Claudia Wu
Colu Henry
Cynthia Samanian
D.J. Blickenstaff
Daniel Calano
Danielle Healy
Debra Cole

Deepa Raj
Devra Ferst
Doel Kar
Don Reed
Donna Yen
Edita Robinson
Eleanore Park
Elizabeth Tilton
Emily Miller
Emma Orme
Eno Sarris
Gargi Ratnaparkhi
Hannah Hoyt and Kenny Polyak
Henry Goldberg
Hirsh Elhence
Iris Liu
Isha Elhence
Iva Dixit
Jacque Ostrom
James Lee
Jamie Sholder
Jean Mason and Anamika Goyal
Jeb Waters
Jenna Lieberman (and her book club!)
Joanna Sciarrino
Jodie Roussell
John Hornbeck
Kaitlyn Spong
Karen Peterson

Kat Johnson
Kat Kinsman
Katie Young
Kay O'Laughlin
Khushbu Shah
Ki Mae Heussner and Rohit Gupta
Kimberly Rubin
Kristie Chan
Laurel Stutsman
Lauren and Greg Keches
Liane Smith
Ligaya Mishan
Lila Battis
Lindsay Ellis
Lindsay Haut
Liz Pierson
Luisa Sperry and Michael Adelman
Mackenzie Kelley
Maggie Fulton
Maia Matsushita
Malia Litman
Margaret Jessiman
Marguerite Mariscal
Marian Bull
Matthew and Amanda Peterson
Max Falkowitz
Megha "Appachi" Motgi
Melissa Fulton

Monica Dutia
Morgan Blackburn
Nadia Chaudhury
Nadia Tamby
Nupur Grover
Olivia Terenzio
Patricia Lee
Phyllis Quach
Priya Desai
Priyanka Naik
Rachna Elhence
Rebecca Palkovics
Remy Fine
Roopa Kalyanaraman Marcello
Ruby Blum
Ruchir Elhence
Ryan Beiermeister
Ryan Healey
Sahanna Bhatt
Sam Gutiérrez
Sam Shore
Sameer Deshpande
Sara Stone
Sarah Jampel
Sarah Smith
Saurabh Bhardwaj
Serena Anis
Shivani Bhatia
Sonia Chopra
Sophie Stevenson

Stephen Praetorius
Sue Chan
Sumeet Garg
Talene Monahon
Talia Ralph
Tara Hohenberger
Tatiana Gupta and Raghav Gupta

Tejal Rao
Thea Stutsman
Thea Sutton and Jack Boger
Vaidehi Garg
Vicky Stein
Victoria Li
Wei Tchou

Maria Qamar is an award-winning author and artist who saw her social following skyrocket after publishing Desi pop art on her Instagram page, @hatecopy. From there, her book, *Trust No Aunty*, a collection of graphic panels retelling her childhood with a socially conservative upbringing and her battle against racism and misogyny, led her to further popularity. She has built a significant following on social media and garnered interest from media outlets across the country, such as *Vogue*, *Harper's Bazaar*, Google, Buzzfeed, and more. She continues to build a name for herself not only as a renowned content creator but also as one of the creative eyes behind the set of *The Mindy Project*. Prior to her rise to fame, she worked as a copywriter at a Toronto ad agency.

About the illustrator

Mackenzie Kelley, aka @mackannecheese, is based in Austin, Texas. Her work is geared toward storytelling through documentary portraiture and food, often brought to light at theworldinapocket.com, an online project devoted to celebrating the dumplings of the world and the people who make them. Mack was pregnant during the photo shoot for *Indian-ish*, and her firstborn fell in love with chhonk on everything before she was even born.

About the photographer

Index

"A great starter book for anyone who has ever wondered how to make basic Indian food in an American kitchen. Priya and Ritu's methods are approachable, easy to execute, and employ everything from microwaves to Instant Pots, because that is the way most Americans do things now."

—From the foreword by PADMA LAKSHMI, host/executive producer of Bravo's *Top Chef* and author of the *New York Times* best-selling *Love, Loss, and What We Ate*